TechnoTeaching

TAKING PRACTICE TO THE NEXT LEVEL IN A DIGITAL WORLD

Julie M. Wood
Nicole Ponsford

HARVARD EDUCATION PRESS

Cambridge, Massachusetts

Library of Congress Control Number 2013952615

Paperback ISBN 978-1-61250-679-1
Library Edition ISBN 978-1-61250-680-7

Published by Harvard Education Press,
an imprint of the Harvard Education Publishing Group

Harvard Education Press
8 Story Street
Cambridge, MA 02138

Cover Design: Wilcox Design
Cover Image: © iStock.com/liangpv

The typefaces used in this book are ITC Slimbach, ITC Stone Sans, ITC Weidemann, Vandijk, and Calibri

Contents

FOREWORD

Julie Wood and Nicole Ponsford have given a wonderful gift to all the teachers out there who experience daily apprehension—even guilt—about their reluctance to enter the digital teaching age. What's the gift? A manual that will help them overcome their feelings of inadequacy as they learn how to transform technology from an enemy into a friend—a friend capable of helping any teacher achieve that elusive goal of helping students enhance their learning, thinking, and language skills on the way to deeper disciplinary knowledge.

As such, this is a book that meets head-on the challenges presented to U.S. teachers by the Common Core State Standards (CCSS) for English language arts. We know that these standards put skills and strategies to work in the quest for acquiring deep disciplinary knowledge of the sort inscribed in the domains of literature, science, and history. We know that the odds-on favorite framework for promoting CCSS thinking, reading, and writing is project-based learning. We know that technology is featured in the standards and in the assessments being built to measure their mastery. And finally, with this book, we have a theory, a set of principles of practice, and some well-developed cases to show us how to manage the kind of pedagogy and assessment that will promote progress toward the CCSS.

But the real genius of the book has nothing to do with these new standards. That's just a side benefit stemming from the book's serendipitous appearance in 2014. That's not why Julie and Nicole wrote the book. Instead, they wrote it to inspire all teachers, from the reluctant neophyte to the self-proclaimed nerd, to avail themselves of the affordances of the ever-expanding set of digital tools that is increasingly available to teachers AND, even more important, to students in today's schools. Let me underscore the phrase, **to students**! The fact that today's students arrive in our classrooms as digital natives means that those of us who aspire to be teachers don't really have the option of focusing exclusively on traditional media in our subject matter courses. As important and useful as books and paper are as tools of literacy and learning, we do our students a disservice if we don't assist them in learning how to negotiate that subject matter within the new media available in today's world—and with the new literacies that come with those new media.

Of course, there is a certain irony in Julie and Nicole's effort—communicating to the rest of us about the virtues of the digital journey through the medium of conventional print! But we'll forgive them that self-contradiction because we know that they would not have been able to reach a large part of their teacher audience if they had chosen to convey their message in a digital medium. Why? Because the very teachers Julie and Nicole most want to reach might not ever find the information they need to make the transformation if it were available only in a digital format.

Print on paper is about the only thing conventional about the book. It possesses some wonderful affordances that make Julie and Nicole's message all the clearer and friendlier. First, they convey all their "information" in a decidedly and cleverly narrative style. In fact, they create three fictitious teachers, Melissa, Zayid, and Jasmine, each representing a "composite" teacher with a dramatically different stance toward technology—the reluctant neophyte, the user, and the technophile, respectively. We meet these hybrid personalities in each substantive chapter, and we learn how each of them meets the challenges and issues that are the focus of each chapter. How does each transform her or his best conventional lesson to a digital environment? How does each incorporate language, thinking, and problem solving into a digital experience? And so on. The characters might be fictitious, but not their experiences. They ring true because they are based on a rich set of experiences that Julie and Nicole bring to this book, both as teachers who have made the transformation themselves, and as coaches who work constantly to guide others through that same transformation. Another narrative-like feature of the book that you will encounter in each chapter is the direct voices of the two authors—Jules and Nic, they call themselves in this role, no doubt to give these cameo characters a friendly face. They read like advice columns and appear in sidebars as comments on their own text! Very "meta"! And, more to the point, very useful to teachers as tips in meeting challenges they will encounter along their journey into Techno-Teaching (the term that Julie and Nicole use to distinguish their approach to teaching with digital tools).

We meet each of these distinctive characters (we even learn a bit about their personal lives and food preferences!) as they meander through the agonies and ecstasies of various stages of use—starting out, jumping in, hunkering down, stretching, branching out, and reflecting on the journey. This is a useful literary device, precisely because we get to see what that part of the journey looks like from the decidedly different perspectives of Melissa, Zayid, and Jasmine.

If the tone of the book is teacher friendly, then the focus is decidedly practical. Lots of direct advice about how to think through plans, implement technologies, assess how well students are making their way on the journey (lots of great stuff on formative assessment woven through each chapter), and cope with the novelty of it all. But just because it is practical doesn't mean it isn't grounded in research and theory about teaching and learning. It's clearly grounded in work emanating from the use of technology in the cognitive sciences, and it has many "principles of good teaching" sprinkled through most of the chapters. My favorite principle in the entire book: to make technology work in the classroom, it's not a matter of *using* digital tools but rather a matter of *integrating* the technology into the fabric of the curriculum. It may sound, on the surface, like a minor distinction, but it's not. When technology is integrated, it changes from being a device to get the work done and becomes synergistically related to the curricular goals. You could not imagine achieving the curricular goals without the technology.

Who's the audience? That's pretty transparent from the very beginning of the book. This is written for any and all teachers, regardless of their level of technological comfort, who are about to take the plunge into the world of

TechnoTeaching. And it will be equally useful to elementary and secondary teachers. The examples and the three composite teachers span the entire K–12 continuum.

I've read a lot of professional books on using computers in the classroom. And I always find them a little flat in affect. I don't come away from them just dying to transform every classroom in America into a digital laboratory. Not so with this book by Julie Wood and Nicole Ponsford! I left my reading of it ready to sign on the dotted line and become an advocate for the kind of teaching and learning they describe in the book. Read it! I bet you will be ready to sign up too.

—P. David Pearson
Professor
Graduate School of Education
UC Berkeley

Introduction

Congratulations, your school has just purchased a cart housing twenty-four tablet computers. Your principal or headmaster wants you to roll it right into your classroom and start innovating—tomorrow.

Or you are a fairly advanced edtech teacher, but your career is stalled in second gear. Maybe you were recently passed over for an instructional coordinator position. While your colleagues know you are keen on using new gadgets with pupils, they have absolutely no idea how innovative you really are, because you are uncomfortable being in the spotlight. You could be a positive force for change, but you secretly fear that it will seem as though you are showing off, making your colleagues' practice seem antiquated by comparison. (And maybe it is!)

Perhaps you read all the blogs and belong to several online groups specifically geared to edtech enthusiasts. There is so much amazing stuff out there! Yet, if you are honest with yourself, you might realize that you tend to hop from gadget to gadget and app to app. While your students may be engaged in learning, you may have allowed your excitement over the *new new thing* to take precedence over a meaningful connection with your curriculum.

Or again, maybe you are an edtech professional development expert. Although you believe you have found your calling, you find it tricky to work with educators who are all over the map when it comes to edtech integration.

How can you possibly design workshops and other events that will be valuable for everyone, regardless of where they are on the TechnoTeaching continuum?

Or maybe you are a school leader. Many members of your staff are technology enthusiasts. You have some funds that you could dedicate to purchasing new digital equipment. But where to begin? So far, nobody has convinced you that the tools in question will improve student learning or test scores. Nor has anyone shown you a proposed budget.

Sound familiar?

OUR MISSION

Our mission in writing this book is to reach out to every teacher who is an idealist at heart, but isn't sure how to reenvision his or her practice in the digital age.

It's for every teacher who has had everything go haywire when teaching a lesson involving educational technologies.

It's for every teacher who wants to level the playing field for his students, empowering them in twenty-first-century terms, but has barely enough money in the budget for crayons and construction paper.

It's for every teacher who wants to innovate with tech tools, but keeps hearing from those around her that it's impossible to do it well. She not only wants to do it brilliantly, but she'd also like to share her success stories with others, beyond geographical boundaries. She realizes that today's students are global citizens (many are multilingual) and wants to give them every opportunity to engage with peers all over the planet.

It's for every formerly well-respected master teacher who now feels like a dinosaur waiting for that asteroid to strike. He knows that change didn't happen overnight, yet somehow the digital revolution feels so sudden.

If you are holding this book in your hands, you have come to the right place. This book is for *you*.

Our goal in writing this book is threefold. First, we aim to show how all teachers can kick their practice up a notch by integrating technology with best practices into teaching and learning. We call this *TechnoTeaching*. This approach is for every teacher, regardless of whether you are a novice who has made only a few brave forays into teaching with technology, or you are at the vanguard of promoting pioneering twenty-first-century practices in your community (and perhaps even the larger world).

This approach will also help U.S. teachers align their instruction with the Common Core State Standards (CCSS). Under these guidelines, every teacher needs to incorporate literacy instruction into every subject area. Also, the creative and effective use of digital media is no longer optional; beginning in kindergarten, children are now expected to use new tools both to become literate citizens and to broaden their understanding of the world. This book will help you hone your skills. It will also help you prepare your students to be "college and career ready in writing, speaking, listening, and language," consistent with CCSS guidelines.[1]

Second, we aim to show you how to help narrow the persistent race- and income-based achievement gap in today's schools by giving *all* students the opportunity to use multimedia and communicate what they have learned with others near and far. We have all too often seen how budget cuts affect low-income schools. Many children are denied access to the tools they will need to be successful members of society in twenty-first-century terms. We will also suggest ways for you to provide rich language experiences, such as online vocabulary development tools and multimedia programs, for your pupils who are learning English.

Third, we strive to help narrow the digital divide by providing all students with an equal chance to succeed in our technological world. Research shows that children in more affluent communities not only have a plethora of digital tools and gadgets to experiment with, but they are also shown how to use them—not with drill-and-practice routines (as in lower-income schools), but in real-world applications like solving geometry problems, designing fashions, or flying an airplane (virtually).[2] The question of how to redress these types of inequities is foundational to the ideas we present in this book. If you agree, then read on.

WHAT HAPPENS WHEN TWO EDUCATORS MEET IN CYBERSPACE?

How we "met" is testament to how our lives are impacted by advancing technology. Nicole—an award-winning multimedia teacher, school leader, and coach from Britain—was interested in expanding her client base as an online consultant. She decided to post a biography on LinkedIn to see what would happen. Julie—an experienced teacher, multimedia designer, and teacher mentor—was keen on making links outside of the United States to learn about education in different cultures. We made sure our top halves looked presentable, in true news anchor style, and "met" on Skype (both pretending that we did this every week).

We discovered a lot of common ground, despite our differences. We talked about teachers, professional development, the economy and its impact on schools, and how eager teachers are to update their practice. After our chat and several e-mail exchanges, we realized that it doesn't matter where you are on the globe or what experience you have: teaching in the twenty-first century is both exciting and problematic.

What was interesting for us was the fact that we discussed only education, not family or friends. This came later. We were both focused upon the same subject. We wanted to work out a way to become smarter at integrating digital media into educationally rich projects. We were both often dismayed by what passed for innovation in schools. To our thinking, there was too much hype about cool new tools and how quickly children figure out how to use them, without any serious regard for the nature of schools and what decades of research (along with current research on the brain) have taught us about how children learn.

We talked it over and decided to find a way to join forces. We believed that being from different cultures, as well as having come of age at different times in history, would be a boon. Nicole was born in a time of great technological advancement, while Julie grew up thinking 33.3 rpm Beatles albums were the greatest invention ever. In Nicole's time we have created the International Space Station, while Julie remembers the excitement of the *Apollo 11* space flight that landed men on the moon. Despite these differences, we have one big thing in common: an abiding passion for helping all children succeed as learners. We also share a passion for helping teachers and administrators use every tool at hand to create schools in which teaching and learning can flourish. We are both at times puzzled by what we see in today's schools and society at large: techno-blur. Learning without frontiers? E-learning? Digital studies? Transmedia? The jargon alone is bewildering. We wonder how it all fits into our vision of how schools need to evolve to stay current (and relevant) in the digital age.

Above all, we wanted to use our combined knowledge, experience, and skills to help teachers whose attempts at edtech integration feel like a white-knuckle rollercoaster ride.

So, where to begin?

THE CHALLENGE

We had lots of ideas to start with. But one idea kept jumping to the forefront: *all* teachers use technology to some degree, but not all teachers are where they want to be. *They are not yet TechnoTeachers.* Technology is there in the classroom, but for some it is a priority, for others an add-on. Some teachers use it for impact in their lessons (student engagement or lesson criteria). Some use it for bells and whistles. Some try to hide it in cupboards. Many get sidetracked by focusing on learning the next new thing in digital tools. Many do not stop to reflect how technology is (or is not) helping students as learners. They are not sure of their role as a member of a global community.

We concluded that there were three elements to using educational technology well. The first element is *Skills & Tools*. Being a *skill*-ful teacher means knowing how to use a variety of digital tools and gadgets—or, as importantly, knowing where to go to learn how to use them. These Skills & Tools might include editing and manipulating photographs, creating videos and documentaries, using interactive whiteboards, finding and archiving digital resources on the Internet, and creating digital books using online tools. Teachers who are tech savvy make it a point to stay on top of "the latest," whether that involves updating the operating system on their computers or learning their way around Google Docs. The element of Skills & Tools also includes being able to access resources and support systems for students that can help *them* learn new skills with the tools that are within their reach.

The second element is *Content*. What subject areas form the basis of a teacher's curriculum? What ideas are administrator's or teacher professional developer's trying to get across? Content refers to essential subject matter, the gist of teaching and learning throughout the school year. Content is substrata. The big ideas that teachers aim to get across during a given school year. Without Content, using edtech can result in "fun episodes" in learning random information.

But without a positive attitude toward teaching and learning with digital tools, the first two elements are all for naught. What good are the Skills & Tools if a teacher uses them only to check the weather app on his iPad or play *Star Wars* games? What good is content knowledge in the twenty-first century without a willingness to set aside faded lecture notes and have students launch their own investigations using a wealth of online resources? Thus we came up with what we call *Mindset*, the third element of TechnoTeaching. Mindset refers to being willing to be a pioneer (and even a bit of a guinea pig). It means being willing to give up on perfection and teach a lesson involving a new skill *at the same time* that students are learning it. It means being willing to set aside traditional ways of doing things even when it's scary. It means reaching out to colleagues so no one is ever out on a limb all alone. It means taking risks and engaging in continuous learning and reflection so that students are prepared to assume their role as global citizens.

Coming up with the three elements of TechnoTeaching led to a Eureka moment. We saw in a flash that regardless of what kind of technology is being used, or how much of it, the most skillful teachers—the ones making the greatest impact on student engagement and learning—are *able to weave together all three of these elements*.

More typically, the elements of TechnoTeaching play out unevenly. A teacher weak in Mindset (that grumpy, cynical one in the corner) might work in a very well-resourced school with an excellent professional development program (Skills & Tools and Content). The enthusiastic (Mindset), geeky (Skills & Tools) teacher might not plan his lessons quite as well as he should (Content). Or the department with the very detailed schemes of work (Content) might have one camera for the entire school and be pretty indifferent about the digital revolution (Mindset). What is the implication here? How can this book help?

Another aspect of Skills & Tools, Content, and Mindset to bear in mind is that your students also have strengths and challenges in these areas. We have all worked with the child who is a whiz at learning how to use new gadgets, but enjoys them for their own sake rather than as a learning tool. Other children have great ideas for podcasts but do not yet know how to create them and post them on the class website. Still others have much to offer, but have attentional issues or need help learning to share what they know when working on a project with peers in small groups. In a nutshell, we're all in this together.

OUR SYSTEM

Although we confess to being a bit starry-eyed about this brave new world, we realize that many hurdles await teachers and administrators who aspire to become TechnoTeachers. Many of the challenges involve Skills & Tools, Content, and Mindset. Giving and/or receiving training for building a set of *skills,* based on having opportunities to play around with digital *tools* in this era of rapid change, can be daunting. How do you find time? What about the fact that the tools themselves seem to change hourly (e.g., new operating systems, new ways of storing and retrieving data)?

Also, making sure that the *Content* is driving the use of technology is trickier than it sounds. Many school programs have been criticized for letting "the tail wag the dog," allowing the cool factor to trump learning.

Mindset may be the stickiest wicket of all. Perfectionists need to learn to accept (if not embrace) occasional failure in order to get to the next level; skeptics need to try on a bit of optimism; lone wolves need to build relationships with supportive colleagues; and traditional teachers need to let go sometimes and allow their students to take the lead.

What this book offers is a systematic plan that teachers, school leaders, and staff developers can use to make sure integrating edtech is done right. If you go through the system, you will be tapping into better practice. We've incorporated three universal elements that you can use no matter what gizmo comes along; we designed our system to withstand the test of time.

Our system, drawn on our collective experience mentoring and helping hundreds of teachers to integrate technology into their curriculum, builds incrementally, brick by brick. We begin with your best unit. Then we show you how to plan a total of six (or more if you like) units over the course of the school year. Next we ask you to challenge yourself further through short, dynamic lessons that may take as little time as one class period. We let you know when it is time to reach out to the global community. We provide forms to help you track and then reflect on your progress as you plan ahead for future years.

Throughout, we offer a framework to help you understand the extent to which you are truly *integrating*, rather than merely *using*, new tools. The two approaches are as different as the sea and the stars. While using new tools might win you instant success, *integrating* new tools is what counts. By weaving them into your practice in ways that deepen learning, you will have the most impact as an educator. We will show you how.

To make things more concrete (and fun!) we will describe the joys and sorrows of three fictional teachers as they adopt our system. These teachers—archetypes of teachers we have worked with—have different worldviews, years of experience, and familiarity (and levels of open-mindedness) about integrating new tools into their lessons. Along the way, we will put on our mentor hats and give them advice based on our combined thirty-plus years of helping teachers use more technology in different types of schools, from low-income to affluent settings.

We hope much of what we show you will seem like the times when you and a colleague have a quick, encouraging chat in the corridor, or over a cup of coffee. In some cases, we also imagine this book will be like a professional development event that gives you new ideas for improving your own practice, as well as ways to lead the change.

We imagine that you already know the ins and outs of the subject area guidelines for your particular teaching situation. Similarly, this is not a how-to book for using new tools; simple Google searches and YouTube tutorials will lead you to more up-to-date information than we could ever include between the covers of this guide. We also assume your school leaders have already developed safety guidelines for Internet and social media use in your schools, that you know these policies, and that you have created a positive space for students and have had open, honest discussions about digital citizenship. Key conversation topics include online etiquette, the dangers of cyberbullying, and the importance of maintaining a positive online presence. As many people have discovered, once they have posted a photo or message to a social media website, it is nearly impossible to erase.

THE HUMAN ELEMENT

Again, in the non-starry-eyed department, we acknowledge the downside of living in the digital age. In her book, *Alone Together*, for example, clinical psychologist Sherry Turkle sends a piercing message about where we are headed as a culture, given the strong attachment we have to our devices. What have iPads and iPhones done to our human relationships? Do we spend enough time in face-to-face communication? Are adolescents' identities being shaped by how others perceive them in a virtual space as opposed to real life ("RL," in cyberspeak)? Society has reached a point, Turkle says, where "[W]e fear the risks and disappointments of relationships with our fellow humans. We expect more from technology and less from each other."[3]

Several other educators and psychologists are also fearful about what new gadgets are doing to our brains and our ability to process complex information. Others lament the fact that our children are so enamored of various iPad apps that they have come to think of life as one big collection of them. Still others offer advice on how and when adults should pry children away from their devices (not to mention advising parents on how important it is to put down their cell phones and talk to their children).[4] Where will it all lead (we ask, as smartwatches become the new craze)? What sorts of boundaries do we need to create to keep the human element front and center even as we encourage children to use new tools in rich and rewarding ways? These are some of the questions that have grounded our thinking. They have led us to emphasize the human element of using new tools. While other authors may hyperventilate over new devices, we get excited about how technology-enhanced experiences, like Skyping with peers in another country, can open doors for children, helping them understand the interconnectedness of the world.

While other authors offer you a one-size-fits-all formula to becoming a techno-star overnight, we show you how to reflect on your practice and take it up several notches over time. We offer you step-by-step guidelines for infusing your best curricular units with new technologies, then using these units to anchor the thirty-six weeks of your school year.

By the time you have finished reading this book, you will have learned how to reach deep inside yourself (with help from your colleagues near and far) to become the type of thoughtful, innovative teacher you always wanted to be.

HOW TO USE THIS BOOK

In chapter 1 we begin by sharing the theoretical underpinnings of this book. Beginning with our six basic beliefs about how to help teachers incorporate edtech into their practice, we explain the research and best practices that have grounded our work.

Helping you situate yourself within the TechnoTeaching world and figuring out where you want to go is the aim of chapter 2. We also introduce you to our three fictional TechnoTeachers, archetypal characters who represent a composite of many teachers we have worked with over the years. TechnoWhy? Melissa is a history teacher in a high school in Newport, Rhode Island. Once a closet Luddite, Melissa is finally ready to take the plunge into the digital age, mainly because she realizes that however gifted a teacher she may be, if she does not begin integrating new technologies into her teaching she will be doing her students a major disservice. Her students are skilled and ready to go. While Melissa is an expert in her content, she needs a systematic plan to help her focus on integrating digital tools. She needs to open her mind to new possibilities including those that allow her students the opportunity to take the lead on twenty-first-century projects.

Then there is TechnoOK Zayid, an émigré from Mumbai to Bournemouth, England, who teaches middle school English. Zayid is naturally good with gadgets and loves trying out new apps and software with his students and his two sons. The only problem is that his approach is often too spontaneous and impulsive. It is not sufficiently grounded enough in content to have a significant impact on student learning. He needs a plan to connect his love of using new tools and gadgets in the classroom with his English curriculum and his students' learning profiles (including many English language learners). Can he use iPads to help his students access apps that will be a boon for their writing? Can he adapt software for creating graphic organizers for students who need help structuring a story or article? How can new tools deepen teaching and learning for the adolescents in his classes?

Last, meet TechnoYes! Jasmine, who teaches fourth grade in Québec City. Jasmine has a pioneer's zeal for innovation in her classroom. She was the first in her school to use Skype. She was the first to bend the capabilities of word processing software to improve students' writing. She was the first to use assistive technologies with students with individual needs. What Jasmine has yet to figure out, though, is how to tell the world about her innovative teaching methods. She is ripe for taking on a leadership role both inside her school and beyond, virtually. She is also ready to introduce her students to the online world. She believes that by connecting with peers around the world, her students will be able to reflect on who they are, what is important to them, and how other children see the world. But first she needs a plan to open her students' eyes to the world around them.

In chapter 3, we begin the process of deepening your practice, by designing a single six-week project that we call a Stellar Unit. We show you how our

TechnoTeachers (and you) can take each of their best units and infuse them with new technologies for in-depth, student-centered learning. The process is somewhat messy, just as it is in the real world. We show you how to plan and refine your own technology-rich Stellar Unit.

Taking it a step further, chapter 4 shows how our teachers hunker down and "anchor" their year by mapping out four more Stellar Units using a blueprint model. You will see how our three TechnoTeachers, who are not accustomed to planning this far in advance, take on what we call the "180-Day or 36-Week Challenge." You will also see how they reach out to technology coordinators and instructional technology (IT) specialists for ideas and extra resources.

As a complement to long-range planning, in chapter 5 you will find ideas designed to stretch your TechnoTeaching Skills & Tools, Content, and Mindset. We offer several short-term projects to complement your Stellar Units. Some of them can be completed in a single forty-five-minute class period. You will see how our three fictional teachers are presented with a "dare" to select one of our nine "Dare Devil Missions." Each one rises to the challenge. Then we turn the spotlight on you. Which Dare Devil Mission will be the best fit for you and your students?

We will also dare you to integrate a seasonal short project into your curriculum, such as "Theater and the Arts" and "Holidays Around the World." These projects also involve experimenting with tools such as Google Maps, multimedia software, and astronomy websites.

But is it enough to be a star in your immediate surroundings? Is it enough for your students to work within the confines of their community? Not in this age of globalization. You can help your students become global citizens through the Internet and by using telecommunications tools. In chapter 6, we show you how. Grounded in the theories of international researchers such as Howard Gardner and Marcelo Suárez-Orozco, we explain how connectivity among children and adolescents can be a positive force, helping to eradicate prejudice and cultural misunderstandings. As Sir Tim Berners-Lee, the inventor of the Internet, has expressed it: "Although you can look at the Web as a technical system, perhaps a more reasonable or useful way is to look at it as a system for connecting humanity through technology."[5]

It can be frustrating to create an edtech plan and then not be able to find the resources you need (both financial and human capital) because of budget cuts and other types of financial shortfalls. In chapter 7, we show you how to go after the resources you need to realize your vision. From justifying a budget, to appealing to big business, to writing a grant proposal, we have several ideas to help get you and your students get up and running, if you are willing to be creative and, in a nutshell, *ask*.

As John Dewey and others have pointed out over the last hundred years, excellence in teaching also involves taking the time to reflect on your practice. It is easy to get caught up in the momentum of teaching, leading professional development sessions, or being a tech coordinator with no time to record your lessons through journaling or taking photographs. In chapter 8, we offer several tools to guide your reflective process, assess progress made toward your goals over the year, and make plans for refining your units for the next year.

We begin and end this book with what we call our TechnoTeaching Manifesto (yes, a very formal word, yet we think it fits). It captures our core beliefs as well as the structure of this book.

- *Be bold. Be a dare devil*—no matter where you are on the TechnoTeaching continuum.
- *Build on what you know and care about.* The subject matter you know and are passionate about provides you with the best way to begin your TechnoTeaching journey (i.e., designing your Stellar Units).
- *Plan ahead.* Not simply planning for the next unit, but mapping everything out for an entire school year (i.e., creating a TechnoTeaching blueprint) will reward your time and effort tenfold.
- *Create a support system.* While it is great to have cool gadgets and goodies at your fingertips, your best resource is human capital—the educators you have access to, near and far, who can become part of your

support system, with you giving back by sharing what you have learned (yes, even the disasters).

- *Think globally.* Children growing up in the digital age (whether we call them Generation Zs, digital natives, or millennials) are living in a vastly different world than the one in which we were raised. By teaching them well, and helping them develop a mindset that extends well beyond their immediate world, we can help them become actors on the global stage.

- *Forge ahead.* Not all of your colleagues will embrace the fact that you are working hard to retool your practice. Change is harder for some people than others. (Just look at some of the characters in *Downton Abbey* after World War I—longing for the way life used to be but would never be again.) Keep forging ahead anyway. Even better, try to win over the tech-averse people in your life and get them on your side.

- *Be a leader.* Working at the forefront of technology integration will set you apart. It can be a springboard for you to become an influential educational leader and help motivate you to keep learning, no matter what the "next new thing" is.

- *Have faith.* You are smarter and more resourceful than you think. And once you gain momentum as a TechnoTeacher, there will be no stopping you. Have faith in yourself. We do.

We aim to take you by the hand, every step of the way, pausing to give you that much-needed time to evaluate and personalize the approach. We will help you see what the next level is and how to create goals. Not because it is "cool," but because it will enrich teaching and learning in your classroom. You, and your students, deserve it. You will come to question how and why, measure your progress and, if necessary, have enough confidence to ride against the tide. This is what it means to be a *TechnoTeacher*.

We will offer you advice along the way based on our expertise. Our "Nic advises"/ "Jules advises" sidebars will guide you. We will step outside the teaching experience, press pause, and give you time to catch your breath and reflect.

As mentors, we are still learning. Although we try our best to stay current in a field that is changing by the nanosecond, there are times when an important research paper or innovation does not land on our radar. Like any educator, we sometimes stumble. We have misconceptions. Julie, for example, is not at all certain about the cloud and how her storage locker in the stratosphere can hold her music and documents, next door to the satellite that is home to "Jill," her GPS guide. Nicole is not sure where to start with computer programming. She also wonders if video will replace texting in the near future and what to do about that.

What we can say with all humility is that we have tried to make the Nic advises/Jules advises sidebars not just pie-in-the-sky dreams, but useful ideas derived from the hard-won lessons we have learned along the way.

Let's get started.

FINAL THOUGHT: TECHNOTEACHERS IN CYBERSPACE

What happens if you want more support, ideas, or challenges after this book? Well, we've thought about that too. We would not be TechnoTeachers if we had not built a website, would we?

This book is very much the start of the TechnoTeacher journey. We know that in a short time some of our ideas will need a more contemporary backdrop. Come visit us at our website (www.TechnoTeachers.com) and other forms of social media to read, respond, and add to our newest ideas as part of the online "TechnoTeaching Learning Community." Our aim is to make the website as interactive as possible. Come and share your ideas with others.

Our TechnoTeacher characters will be part of the mix, suggesting weekly missions so you can continue to plan, revise, and reflect upon your work.

Our biggest hope is that you will share your journey with us and help others with their teaching. Together we can keep on learning about learning.

CHAPTER 1

What Is TechnoTeaching?

With all the definitions floating around the blogosphere, you could be forgiven for wondering what exactly *is* a TechnoTeacher. To us, a TechnoTeacher sees the big picture of technology use with learners. He understands that today's children are growing up in a world that is vastly different from the one he knew as a child. He also acknowledges that being literate in today's society means being a savvy user of the myriad gadgets that are part of the fabric of daily life. He knows that children who are not part of this world will have a hard time being successful throughout their academic careers. The link between personal computing and intelligence has been apparent since the 1980s, when microcomputers moved from the office to the home. This shift gave people a sense of ownership, a personal challenge, and perhaps more importantly, ambition to reach to the next level. They could do things they couldn't with traditional devices: pencil and paper are wonderful inventions, but they can take you only so far. Today, the Internet can bring the world to you in a computer (i.e., a smartphone) that fits into your pocket.

We sometimes hear teachers say things like, "My students need to learn the basics. They're not ready to be set loose on computers." Or "I've been teaching for twenty years. I've got it down to a science. Technology will only complicate things." These types of attitudes are roadblocks to learning. They shortchange children, denying them access to the tools they need right now to enrich their learning. They also deny them the tools and skills they will need to be successful in the future, in all aspects of their lives.

In contrast, we hear other teachers say things like, "I've been playing around with a website that would make it easy for kids to write and publish their own books." Or, "There's a great edtech meetup event this weekend. Who wants to join me?" Or, "I want to see the teachers in my district get the training they need to use iPads not as fun gadgets but as educational tools." Comments like these are dead giveaways that you are working with TechnoTeachers. They are the envelope pushers. A few millennia ago, these are the people who would have been the first to use papyrus; their counterparts a few centuries later would have instinctively understood that moveable type would shake up the world order. Likewise, you will find today's TechnoTeachers wherever deep-seated change is taking place in the way we do things in schools.

As innovators, TechnoTeachers understand that today's students are at the vanguard of a global age. Much of the information they receive comes from digital sources. Children will need to not only know how to use these resources and other tools, but also how to adapt them in new and creative ways—no matter what the next new thing turns out to be an hour, a day, or a year from now.

Here's what we know: *today's students are digital learners—and digital learners need smart, forward-thinking, creative TechnoTeachers.*

This chapter explores what it means to be a TechnoTeacher and the beliefs that undergird our system for becoming one. Our ideas are based on current research and our combined experiences working with hundreds of teachers over dozens of years.

WHAT IT MEANS TO BE A TECHNOTEACHER

Innovation-minded educators think about teaching in sophisticated ways. They may not all be whizzes at using technology, but they strive to combine Skills & Tools, Content, and Mindset in ways that we'll describe later in this chapter. Some are new teachers who have grown up with computers and other gadgets. Others may have begun their careers using more traditional methods, but they've always been innovators at heart. Their quest to find the most effective teaching methods has, more often than not, led them to digital tools.

Although TechnoTeachers get excited about trying out the latest ideas in their classrooms and schools, they're not the type to read an article like "50 Ways to Use Smartphones with Kids" and rush to try out a few new ideas without first thinking about their subject matter and their students.

Still other TechnoTeachers began in the classroom, but are now in administrative roles. We have noticed that good school leaders do everything in their power to support and motivate other TechnoTeachers. It becomes their mission.

We have also noticed that TechnoTeachers tend to be analytical thinkers. They are good at stepping back from their classrooms, thinking about their goals, and striving for much more than the "cool factor." The questions that consume them include: *How will this edtech activity advance my teaching goals for this particular group of students? Will this activity encourage students to think more deeply about subject matter? Will it help level the playing field for all students, across socioeconomic divides?*

THE BELIEFS BEHIND TECHNOTEACHING

After describing our backgrounds and experiences to each other, we realized that we share six basic beliefs about the best ways to help teachers incorporate edtech into their practice. Our approach—and the one outlined in this book—is grounded in our belief that our best work as coaches and mentors is not only built on a foundation of high-quality teaching, but is also rooted in research from the academic world that sheds light on "what works."

What are the latest ideas about effective practice in the digital age? Who is pushing the boundaries of twenty-first-century education? How can we use this knowledge to be better teachers—better TechnoTeachers? This chapter focuses on (and ends with) our way of thinking—six basic beliefs that grew out of our own work—and the implications for your practice. Get ready to plan a year of awe-inspiring digital projects.

TechnoTeachers Evolve over Time

How does TechnoTeaching start? When does it all begin? What factors and personality traits need to be in place? In poring over the vast body of literature on teachers and change, we have come to this conclusion: the Ten-Year Apple Classrooms of Tomorrow (ACOT) Study, although published nearly two decades ago, continues to be an invaluable guide for understanding the stages teachers go through as they become comfortable with, and ultimately amazing at, implementing digital tools into their classrooms.[1]

ACOT researchers concluded that teachers typically evolve through five stages: *entry*, *adoption*, *adaptation*, *appropriation*, and *invention* (see table 1.1). Given the opportunity to be mentored, combined with a strong inclination toward risk taking, teachers can progress through these stages fairly rapidly.

How would you situate yourself within these five stages? Are you at the entry stage, immersed in learning how to use iPads, computers, digital cameras, and other tools?

TABLE 1.1   **ACOT stages of technology use** (Adapted)

Stage	Examples of what teachers do
Entry	Learn the basics of using the new technology.
Adoption	Use the new technology to support traditional instruction.
Adaptation	Integrate new technology into traditional classroom practice. Here teachers often focus on increased student productivity and engagement by using word processors, spreadsheets, and graphics tools.
Appropriation	Focus on cooperative, project-based, and interdisciplinary work—incorporating the technology as needed and as one of many tools.
Invention	Discover new uses for technology tools—for example, developing spreadsheet macros for teaching algebra or designing projects that combine multiple technologies.

Reprinted by permission of the publisher. From Judith Haymore Sandholtz, Cathy Ringstaff, and David C. Dwyer, *Teaching with Technology: Creating Student-Centered Classrooms.* New York: Teachers College Press. Copyright © 1997 by Teachers College Press. All rights reserved.

Or have you already figured out the nuts and bolts of these tools and would place yourself at the adoption stage? If so, you are most likely figuring out strategies for how to replace more traditional materials with edtech. Or you may be working at adapting tools for your students so they can be more productive learners.

Perhaps you are a bit more advanced, and are finding ways to appropriate digital media. Teachers at this stage typically use tools not for a one-shot lesson, but for interdisciplinary and project-based activities. They have also learned how to control the tools rather than having the tools control *them*. Teachers who are at the appropriation stage have reached what we refer to as a *TechoTeacher turning point*.[2]

Which leads us to the invention stage. Teachers at this stage are pioneers, inventing ways to use tools to push the boundaries of what they were originally intended for. The teacher who shows young children how to use time-lapse photography to document the lifecycle of a monarch, from chrysalis to butterfly, for example.[3] Or athletes who use Google Maps not just to find locations, but also to chart a bicycling or running route that covers a number of miles/kilometers. Or Dartfish stop-motion animation, which sports teachers can use to monitor and improve physical education techniques.[4] Teachers at this stage tend to jump in with both feet, encouraging students to use tablets, smartphones, and the like to create projects and express their ideas in original ways.

Teachers who are out there on this ledge are focused on helping students *construct* knowledge, rather than simply passing knowledge down to them.[5] If this describes you, our guess is that it took many years for you to arrive at the invention stage, and that blood, sweat, and tears were your constant companions. But here you are. How will you motivate other educators to join you out there on the ledge?

Our own practice bears out this research finding: real change does not happen after a single workshop or the purchase of a cart of laptops for teams of teachers to share. This idea is reflected in the yearlong planning process we will guide you through. Specifically, as you work to incorporate more digital media into your classroom or school, be aware that this is a process, which takes time, experimentation, and a willingness to fail now and then. We will show you how you can get your feet wet by starting small when doing something new. We will also suggest several short projects intended to allow you to push the limits of what you can do with edtech, depending on your students, school, and community.

TechnoTeachers Are Leaders

In addition to the ACOT framework, we have observed time and time again that two additional factors—*leadership* and *reflection*—are critical to becoming an innovative teacher, working at the highest level of integration. In our practice, and consistent with Julie's dissertation research, we are often struck by how often TechnoTeachers take on leadership roles.[6] They look around, see how current practices could be improved, and set about making changes. Being in a leadership role gives them an added measure of authority. As pioneers, they work to effect change. Their willingness to roll up their sleeves and participate in making policy decisions earns them a seat at the table with all the other movers and shakers.

What do we mean when we say someone is a leader? According to educator Howard Gardner, a leader is "an individual who significantly affects the thoughts, feelings, and behaviors of other individuals. Leaders provide leadership in two principal ways: Through the stories they tell; and through the kinds of lives they lead."[7]

In analyzing the genesis of leadership throughout history, Gardner observes that a leader "takes a story that has been latent in the population, or among the members of his or her chosen domain, and brings new attention or a fresh twist to that story."[8] Leaders also behave in a way that makes sense with whatever story they choose to tell.

As authors, we will try to live up to Gardener's definition of leadership in two ways. First, by being leaders ourselves, bringing you three stories—case studies—of teachers who represent a "fresh twist" on how one becomes a pioneer in the edtech world. Second, by using these stories to show how teachers can become leaders by spreading the word—sharing their stories with other educators near and far. Here's to them. To the teachers who say, "Don't worry. I can show you how to do that," or, "I struggled too, and then I did this and my students really took off."

These same leaders are often virtuoso networkers. Reaching out to others beyond their school communities is second nature to them. They are always on the lookout for "something bigger" and people who will keep them on their toes. We will show you how.

Jules advises   Here is one of my favorite quotations by Andrew Hargreaves and Michael Fullan: "All good leadership is a judicious mixture of push, pull, and nudge. This is a sophisticated practice. It's a combination of nonjudgmentalism, not being pejorative about where people are at the beginning, combined with moving them forward . . . In the end, it's best to pull whatever you can, push wherever you must, and nudge all the time."[9]

TechnoTeachers Reflect on Their Teaching to Improve Practice

The ACOT study documented that reflection "is a core principle for supporting technological integration." ACOT researchers found that teachers who work in teams regularly, who continually reflect on their teaching with others, have a better shot at improving their practice than those who work alone in their classrooms with the door closed.[10] Although it seems like an obvious point, we are still surprised by the number of teachers who try to figure everything out all by themselves even when help is readily at hand.

In a sense, this book is about giving you the opportunity to reflect on your practice: zeroing in on what you'd like to try, determining how to fit it into your teaching units, and then sitting down with colleagues to evaluate how it went and set a few goals for the future.

TechnoTeachers Integrate, Not Just Use, Technology

Our thinking has also been influenced by researchers who have studied the difference between merely *using* versus *integrating* technology. TeachBytes, a blog written by Aditi Rao, a technology integration specialist from Houston, offers a helpful summary of this process (see table 1.2). Rao's conception

TABLE 1.2   **Using versus integrating technology (adapted from TeachBytes)**[1]

How teachers sometimes use technology	How TechnoTeachers integrate technology
Teacher uses technology in random, impulsive ways—it may even be an afterthought.	Teacher uses technology in ways that are planned, with purpose and meaning.
Teacher uses technology once in a while in the classroom.	Teacher weaves technology into the fabric of classroom life.
Teacher uses technology for its own sake—because it seems like a cool idea.	Teacher uses technology with a clear eye toward curricular goals and learning goals.
Teacher uses technology to present students with content.	Teacher uses technology to engage students with content.
Teacher is the person who mainly uses the digital tools.	Teacher places the tech tools in students' hands.
Teacher focuses on how to use a new tech tool.	Teacher focuses on using a tech tool to encourage students to think in new ways.
Teacher uses technology to teach lower-order thinking tasks.	Teacher uses technology to inspire students to use higher-order thinking skills.
Students work with technology in isolation.	Teacher uses technology to facilitate collaboration during class time and beyond.
Teacher uses technology for projects where it might be simpler to just use pen and paper.	Teacher uses technology for projects that would be nearly impossible to do without it.
Teacher uses technology to deliver information.	Teacher uses technology to help students actively construct knowledge.
Teacher uses technology in the margins, like a side order of French fries.	Teacher uses digital tools in ways that are at the heart of learning.

1. Cited in Jeff Dunn, "12 Ways to Integrate (Not Just Use) Technology in Education," http://edudemic.com/2013/04/integrate-technology-in-education/.
Reprinted with permission.

of what it means to integrate technology is reflected later in this book. You will see how our TechnoTeachers use digital tools for formative assessment, group learning and conferencing, and creating culminating projects. You will also see how the type of projects we have designed for teachers to step up their practice are aligned with these ideas.

Take a minute to reflect on *your* approach. Mentally check off the boxes that apply to you. You may find that you are *using* more than *integrating* technology into your teaching. If so, use this new insight as a jumping-off point for improving your practice. Also, bear it in mind as you work through the planning activities in this book.

Nic advises If you haven't had an opportunity to observe technology integration firsthand, consider taking a professional day to visit a school that has built a reputation for innovative practices. Even if the teachers you observe are still finding their way, having the chance to observe them and debrief them afterward will give you a new perspective on TechnoTeaching.

Jules advises Leaders/administrators, encourage your staff to expand their world. Get them out of their comfort zones, working with others—both inside and outside your school environment. Make it easy for them to attend (online or in person) international edtech conferences and other professional development events. Make sure to give them time to share what they have learned with their fellow teachers, even if you can set aside only a few minutes during a faculty meeting. Encouraging your teachers to think more globally is one of the best investments you can make for improving the quality of teaching and learning in your district.

TechnoTeachers Are Guided by Professional and Curriculum Standards

In writing this book we drew from two international sources: the International Society of Technology Educators (ISTE) and the International Reading Association (IRA).[11] Both organizations have asked experts from all over the world to create guidelines for using technology to promote learning.

You will see how our fictional TechnoTeachers try to align their work with the six goals ISTE has created for students (2007). Called the National Educational Technology Standards, or NETS, they are aimed at helping children be productive members of an increasingly technological world. NETS for Students outlines the sorts of procedural knowledge students need to acquire in learning new tools (e.g., selecting and using various applications). ISTE standards also chart a course for teaching students how to become creative, collaborative, critical consumers of information, and problem solvers in the digital age.

Our work is also aligned with the IRA's position paper titled "New Literacies and 21st-Century Technologies." The IRA is committed to the goal of having all teachers integrate information and communication technologies (ICTs) into their practice. It also believes that students deserve the following advantages:[12]

- Teachers who use ICTs skillfully for teaching and learning
- Peers who use ICTs responsibly and who share their knowledge
- A literacy curriculum that offers opportunities for collaboration with peers around the world
- Instruction that embeds critical and culturally sensitive thinking into practice
- Leaders and policy makers who are committed advocates of ICTs for teaching and learning
- Equal access to ICTs

Also reflected in our writing are the Common Core State Standards (CCSS), of which most have been adopted by forty-five states and the District of Columbia. The CCSS exams test students on various aspects of digital literacy, from nuts-and-bolts procedures to being able to evaluate the legitimacy of the information they find online. Many educators are surprised to learn that children as young as kindergarteners are expected to publish their work using digital tools.

Essentially, the Common Core standards for literacy development address the following areas for teachers of every subject, promoting the idea that literacy is essential to academic achievement in all areas:

- Reading literature
- Reading information texts
- Speaking: discussion
- Speaking: presentation
- Listening
- Writing
- Academic language

Read on to see how you can weave the CCSS literacy goals into your curriculum. Discover how you can integrate new tools to deepen and enrich learning, whether your goal is for students to read literature or to discuss their ideas with others in their class (through podcasts and blogs, perhaps) and beyond (through telecommunications tools).

As of this writing, in the U.K. a set of guidelines for educators is in development. We will keep an eye on new developments and post updates on our website as they evolve.

Our approach is heavily influenced by best practices in the areas just named and focuses primarily on literacy. However, in the digital age, every teacher of every subject needs to be concerned with showing students how to read, write, and communicate their work and ideas effectively. Even teachers of math and science can use our framework; it is easy to adapt to content area curricula. The same holds true for educators who teach in arts and humanities departments.

TechnoTeachers Combine Skills & Tools, Content, and Mindset

There is a final step to becoming a TechnoTeacher when it comes to integrating theory and practice. In schools—regardless of where they are—moving to the next level of practice when using technology requires attention to three different aspects of teaching at once: Skills & Tools, Content, and Mindset. The single most important goal for you in becoming a TechnoTeacher is to factor in all three of these elements for every unit you teach. When Skills & Tools align with curricula, teaching becomes student-centered. When you enjoy teaching and believe your students are learning more than ever, your mindset will become even more positive and innovative. This belief is central to our approach, as we show in figure 1.1.

Here is an example of how the synergy among Skills & Tools, Content, and Mindset will allow you to use technology and digital media creatively. Imagine a middle school teacher who begins by learning how to build a website. He figures out the best *tools* to use (e.g., a free drag-and-drop website builder such as Weebly). Before he knows it, his pupils have gained the *skills* they need to build pull-down menus and add video clips.[13] Now they have a functioning website with introductory information about who they are and where their school is located. They are ready to go. But what *content* will they post? Their own short stories? Photography? Information about their basketball and (Jules says) soccer or (Nic says) football teams? Science fair projects? The teacher takes a vote. The idea of having the class create their own virtual photography museum wins. Students are completely immersed in the project. Their teacher notices that he is just as excited about building the virtual museum as they are. He feels invigorated. Other teachers and school leaders begin thinking of him as an innovator. The local newspaper, in fact, runs a short feature article about the virtual photography museum. The teacher's *mindset* has moved up few notches. He is already thinking about the next edtech challenge.

This is the way it can work. The three areas can intersect, with the whole being greater than the sum of its parts.

We are realistic. We know there can be frustrations and tensions here. You may have the Skills, but not the Tools. Your school may have next to no budget and you are currently working on ways to refresh your ICT suite, as no one else seems interested. The lesson Content is solid, but dull as dishwater. Or, even more daunting, you are expected to teach an exciting, well-resourced unit, written by a new member of the staff. Small problem: he has left the school and is now teaching on a remote island. How on earth are you going

FIGURE 1.1   **TechnoTeaching framework**

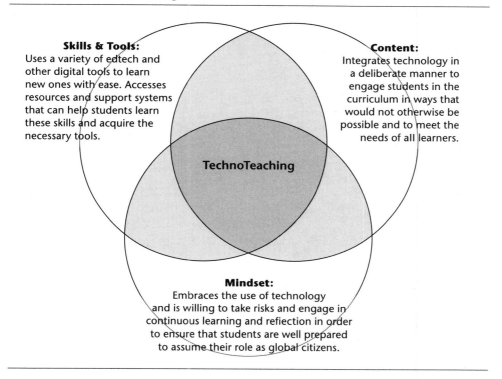

Skills & Tools:
Uses a variety of edtech and other digital tools to learn new ones with ease. Accesses resources and support systems that can help students learn these skills and acquire the necessary tools.

Content:
Integrates technology in a deliberate manner to engage students in the curriculum in ways that would not otherwise be possible and to meet the needs of all learners.

TechnoTeaching

Mindset:
Embraces the use of technology and is willing to take risks and engage in continuous learning and reflection in order to ensure that students are well prepared to assume their role as global citizens.

to build on his unit—especially if you are not quite of the TechnoTeaching *Mindset* yet?

As we progress through the book, you will encounter three TechnoTeachers (Melissa, Zayid, and Jasmine) on their separate journeys in planning and executing a yearlong plan to deepen their practice. Along the way, we will also ask *you* to contemplate how they (and you) consider goals related to Skills & Tools, Content, and Mindset. How do they learn to use new Skills & Tools to deepen their practice and help all students learn to the best of their ability?

But first things first: let's meet our characters and work out which type of TechnoTeacher *you* are.

CHAPTER 2

Starting Out

Where You Are and Where You Want to Go

Now that you have read *our* thinking behind TechnoTeaching, we need to bring these ideas into the real world of teachers—into schools, classrooms, and the principal's or headmaster's office.

In this chapter, you will assess your use of edtech in terms of Skills & Tools, Content, and Mindset. You will also begin to set some goals that will guide you down the path to TechnoTeaching. Along the way, we will introduce our three archetypal teachers as a way of helping you reflect on your practices. These characters are a composite of all the teachers we have mentored and worked with over many years, in both the U.S. and U.K. We want to assure you that we understand where you are coming from, and more importantly, where you want to go. We will use our experience to help you get there.

As you read the story of these teachers—Melissa, Zayid, and Jasmine—you may feel you embody all three to various degrees. Think about how and when that's true. *When has the idea of using digital tools made you break into a cold sweat? When were you courageous? What challenges have you faced in addressing the needs of all of your students?*

Bear these experiences in mind as you read and consider whether any aspects of their teaching style, beliefs, or classes resonate with you, as you read their descriptions and get to know them. By analyzing their work, you will gain insights about your own practice and how to notch it up to the next level.

Consider how our archetypal teachers mix Skills & Tools, Content, and Mindset as they sometimes simply *use* technology, and other times *integrate* it. Then think about how *you* do it.

Each description begins with a general summary of teachers at a particular level: TechnoWhy?, TechnoOK, and TechnoYes! Consider which category applies to you, and feel free to agree/disagree with the characters. (We will meet you on the other side—see you soon.)

THE TECHNOWHY? TEACHER

You really try to avoid technology at all costs, but feel like someone is going to find you out—soon. You do use the computer at home, when no one else is watching, but not in front of people in your department. You know how to use a fax machine, but blogging and Bluetooth are nonsensical words in your mind.

You would like to have new technologies explained to you, but don't want to take the time to learn—time that you could be using to plan your lessons.

Besides, traditional teaching methods have worked well for you over your career. Your students read many books and articles, compose their thoughts in their notebooks, and participate in class discussions. Why try to retool your practice now when there are so many other responsibilities nipping at your heels?

While you're not a Luddite (you would be lost, literally, without a GPS guiding your car), you know how to be a creative teacher without adding digital tools to the equation.

So far, so good. But lately you've noticed that your fellow teachers are making pointed remarks about this being the twenty-first century and how we all need to adapt.

Case Study: Melissa

Melissa glides out of the pool after finishing her morning laps and pulls off her goggles. She glances at the racing clock on the wall as she towels off—only a half-hour to shower, get dressed, and bike the last mile to the high school where she teaches.

Once in the locker room, Melissa notices other women checking their cell phones underneath a poster that shows a cell phone crossed out by a big, red X. One or two women make guilty, whispered calls. Melissa looks on in a bemused way. *People are so addicted to their gadgets! Afraid to be "off the grid" long enough for a workout and shower.* She gives the offenders a conspiratorial grin as she shrugs her workout bag over her shoulder and hurries outside.

Melissa thinks about her upcoming classes as she rides her bicycle down windy roads to the modern wood-and-glass high school where she teaches. Once inside her classroom, she wolfs down an energy bar, then stands at her doorway to greet students.

Today alone, 175 adolescents will enter her classroom over seven class periods. Two students, in separate classes, have been designated as hearing impaired. Some students will be eager to learn history, social studies, and geography. Included in this group will be those who have been identified as gifted and talented. Other students will be a little more challenging to motivate. Some will excel on the formal tests Melissa is required to give each year, while others will be hard-pressed to identify all seven continents on the map. This gap in student achievement frustrates Melissa. She believes with every molecule of her being that it is her job to make sure every student learns the curriculum—and so much more about the world and how it works.

Yet Melissa's idealism is tempered by experience. This is her twenty-first year teaching high school in Newport, Rhode Island. Earlier in her career she began a PhD program in European studies at a university in Boston, but put her degree on hold when her twin daughters were born.

Within her community, Melissa is seen as someone who is tough but fair. She is considered an expert in her content, and over the years she has mentored scores of young teachers in the humanities department and chaired more committees than anyone can count. Despite Melissa's casual look, bicycling down the school driveway, her students have discovered that her backbone is made of steel.

Lately, Melissa has had a nagging sense that as strong a teacher as she is, and however much her students respect her, she is becoming a dinosaur. The times, they are a-changing, but not her. Not yet.

Melissa's fears escalate when she finds out that the principal has decided to move toward a paperless system to conserve resources. Paperless? That would mean she'd have to go digital and upgrade her skills. Stegosaurus alert!

Currently, Melissa's teaching assistant takes care of most of her e-mailing and creates Microsoft Word documents for her (developing content on her own laptop). Melissa has learned to gather and analyze data from senior management, but feels that she would not be able to create a document or spreadsheet from scratch.

Lately, Melissa is starting to rethink her mindset. One of her daughters, Daisy, has offered to help. Daisy has almost convinced her mother that technology would make her life a lot simpler. For starters, Melissa could better keep track of her lecture notes and assignments from year to year in digital files that could be stored on a flash drive, taking up almost no space. "But I've always used paper," says Melissa. "Big, bulky cabinets full of file folders and paper! They're my anchor." Daisy is starting to wonder if it is fear or if her mother is just being lazy.

Melissa hasn't confided in anyone about her fear of being left behind. She's too embarrassed. Instead, she stands at her doorway to greet her students and banter with them about last night's soccer game. Students know to stash their digital gadgets in their backpacks to avoid having them confiscated during class.

Melissa needs help in becoming a twenty-first-century teacher. Although she is strong in content, she needs help with learning digital skills and in adopting the kind of mindset that will allow her students to take ownership of their own learning. She needs to reach out to her fellow teachers. She also needs a TechnoTeaching mentor. Any ideas?

THE TECHNOOK TEACHER

You may not be the teacher with the most PCs or Macs in your classroom, but you do what you can with the technology you have. You use Facebook for socializing with friends outside of the classroom, and can get students around the interactive whiteboard when you want to. You are interested in new technologies, but have no idea how to set up a blog or use video gaming to meet an assessment objective.

But learning how to use techie tools and gadgets comes easily to you. You can always figure out how things work and almost never have to crack open the dreaded manual. And yet, you feel you are missing something. Some elusive quality that would move your TechnoTeaching from fun and novelty to something deeper. Something that had greater impact on all of your students, not just those who get excited about trying out clickers, online surveys, or blogs. Something that would impact student learning in ways both deep and profound.

You'd also like to share the tech-based projects your students have done with your peers, but you don't want people to think you're a show-off. Worse yet, you don't want them to see how much the projects just skim the surface of the curriculum (Content). Your approach lacks vision. You need a plan.

Case Study: Zayid

Zayid drops off his six- and eight-year-old sons at school, runs after them with the lunchboxes they left in the backseat, and then flips on the jazz radio station. A saxophone player in his spare time, Zayid collects his thoughts on the way to school as he listens to Johnny Dankworth.

Yes! Zayid finds a parking space in the crowded faculty lot in front of the 1960s modernist structure where he teaches. He grabs his briefcase. It feels heavy. No wonder—one of his sons has stuffed a toy robot in between his laptop and his papers. He smiles and arranges the robot in a sitting position on the dashboard for the boys to discover when he picks them up.

Zayid grew up in Mumbai, India. His first experience in the U.K. was at university at Oxford, where he majored in English literature. After earning his degree, he became a middle school teacher in a school on the south coast. This is his ninth year teaching English in the same school. He teaches one hundred fifty students a day, with twenty-five or more bursting through his doorway at fifty-five-minute intervals, interrupted only by a forty-five-minute lunch break on most days.

Although many of Zayid's students were born in this country, about 10 percent are immigrants, with Polish, a range of Pakistani languages (including Urdu, Punjabi, Bengali, and Gujarati), and Arabic being the primary home languages. Some are fluent in their native language and English, while others are new arrivals who are just beginning to learn English (termed *English language learners*, or ELLs, in the U.S., and *English as an additional language*, or EALs, in the U.K.). Several other students fall somewhere in between. He knows from firsthand experience what it is like not to speak the same language as those around you. To sit in a classroom not knowing what is happening. To have friends who "miss" the lesson in order to translate it for you and get annoyed as you slowly try to learn customs and new ways. Zayid knows what it's like to be embarrassed by your parents because they don't speak the same language as your friends' parents—and don't want to. He knows what it is like to wish that everyone spoke only one language around the world, just as many of his students do every morning as they get ready for school.

Zayid realizes that he should probably integrate technology in more thoughtful ways for his students. He would be interested in learning how to deepen and extend his lessons by creating engaging projects. For now, he spends far too much time marking papers and doing administrative work to think very hard about it. He is lucky in that his school has access to new technology (he has heard that one teacher uses his mobile phone in lessons and would like to try it). But he is not really sure who can help him figure it out.

Zayid likes to experiment. Although he uses his interactive whiteboard more as a projector than a creative learning space, he has had success with introducing educational websites to his students. The sites tend to be the popular ones. He isn't really sure where to find websites that are more tailored to his curriculum, or the best new blogs where English teachers swap ideas.

An avid Facebook user with his friends, Zayid has not been on Twitter. He Skypes with his sister in Mumbai and always involves his sons so they can get to know their aunt. He has shown his mum how to Skype as well.

Although Zayid has not used a webcam in school, he knows there is a camera in the computer lab if he wants to use it. He downloads most of his resources from a free resource site.

As for his own gadgets, Zayid has a smartphone and a game console, which he uses most nights at home with the boys. He thinks he is doing okay, but would like to be a bit more "whizzy," like the "cool teachers." His peers describe him as someone who stands there, holding up a butterfly net, hoping to catch the next innovation as it flits past.

In his more introspective moments, Zayid realizes that his teaching style may be a little too spontaneous. While his classroom is often a hotbed of learning, Zayid often has no real plan beyond a particular curricular lesson on any given day.

Nonetheless, Zayid's peers hope some of his charisma will rub off on them. They've started a new lunchtime series focused on e-teaching, and asked him to present a few ideas. He feels like too much of an imposter to take them up on their invitation. He'd rather hear about what his peers are doing. Maybe they could help him be methodical and rethink his approach—not just dabbling in the margins, but engaging in a deep and profound way.

Meanwhile, Zayid keeps falling into the same trap of seizing upon "the next new thing" he reads about on educational websites (Google Earth is the latest). But he knows that a more transformative approach to teaching is just within his grasp.

Like Melissa, Zayid could be twice as effective if he joined forces with other teachers. He is strong in skills and tools—learning how to work new gadgets poses no barrier to him. But he needs help in aligning technology with content and his students' learning needs. He needs to adopt a mindset that will allow him to take the time necessary to plan and evolve his practice. Zayid would also benefit from being mentored by someone who understands his style of learning and teaching.

THE TECHNOYES! TEACHER

Do you have a teaching blog or wiki space? Are you on LinkedIn, Twitter, and Facebook, still searching for the ultimate teaching tool?

Are you the teacher who uses your iPhone as a mouse in the classroom? Are you tuned in and plugged into what your digital learners are doing? Are you in frequent communication with them on the bus on the way to school, at lunch, and/or in the evening via smartphones? At the same time, are you tweeting other educators, reading the latest research on young people and media, and sharing some of the innovative teaching practices that have worked for you?

Maybe you are at the stage where you are looking for the next challenge. You might decide to connect with like-minded educators who can help one another constantly improve. You think about becoming an educational leader—both in your school and beyond—but the thought of coaching, writing articles, and presenting at conferences is daunting.

Case Study: Jasmine

Jasmine orders a large cup of coffee at a café in Québec City. Listing a little as she balances her jam-packed laptop bag, she walks the last half-mile to work. The café owners are still yawning as they unfurl their awnings and post the daily specials on the chalkboards. Jasmine pulls a fried egg sandwich out of her bag and gives it to the woman who sits on a park bench every day feeding the birds.

Jasmine is always the first one in the door. The school where she teaches is a nineteenth-century brick structure that houses kindergarten through eighth-grade classes. This is her fifth year teaching fourth grade. She has twenty-eight students, several of whom have individual needs, including one child with diagnosed autism and two with nonspecific learning disabilities.

Jasmine's fiancé also works long hours as an engineer at a software start-up company. They joke about the fact that they are both "geeks." They are also enthusiastic travelers who already have airplane tickets for their honeymoon in Costa Rica.

Today Jasmine plans to begin a new language arts project. Children will act out new vocabulary words from the novels they are reading, take turns video-taping each other (in French and English), and edit their videos. Then Jasmine will post the videos online.

Jasmine takes a deep breath. It is the first time she will be using this technique, which she learned about at a conference. Was she crazy to plan it for today—a day when her principal said he would drop by? What if everything goes horribly wrong? Her stomach tightens as she reheats her coffee in the microwave.

It will be okay, she tells herself. She enjoys taking risks. She was the first in her school to figure out how to teach using tools such as an interactive white-board, tablets, and smartphones. She was also the first to try "flipping the class-room," videotaping several of her math lessons so students could watch them at home on their computers, however many times they wanted. That way, students would come to school having been introduced to a new concept, allowing Jasmine to devote more of the math block to engaging in group problem solving.

Jasmine does have her moments of self-doubt, though. For all her talk about the potential of technology to change teaching and learning, she worries that she hasn't done enough for her academically at-risk students. She knows the other teachers look up to her, but doesn't just want to be a "bells and whistles" teacher. Has she really adapted digital tools to help her students with individual needs learn the curriculum? Not really. Has she found effective strategies to use with her three students who have behavioral issues—strategies that will get their parents involved as well? Well . . . that is her next "growth opportunity," as her principal likes to say.

As a member of the Technology Team at school, Jasmine has designed the school website and blog. She also keeps them up-to-date. Lately, she's been pushing her principal to sign up for a Twitter account so teachers can send parents tweets to remind them about special events. A simple tweet might increase attendance and parental engagement, she points out.

Jasmine uses her own Twitter account in her spare time, and likes to chat with other teachers about how they use technology in their lessons. Many are from the U.K. She also has her own teaching blog, where she shares interesting links with her classes. She uses both Macs and PCs, and has access to both in her school. Jasmine's colleagues (and friends) think she is a digital wizard. They worry, though, that she will get bored with their school and head for "the bright lights" of Silicon Valley.

Jasmine's students see her as the awesome teacher. No idea is too avant-garde to at least talk about. Watch videos to learn how to play chess, then start an afterschool chess club? Sure. Ask a seasoned rock-festival lighting techni-cian to train students how to do it for the school talent show (as Nic once did)? Why not?

Lately, as her friends fear, Jasmine *has* become restless. She daydreams about creating a portfolio of all her projects so she can get her work out there. Maybe she should become an edtech coach. Or a school leader in a cutting-edge school that emphasizes twenty-first-century skills. Or a lead teacher at a virtual school . . .

Jasmine's ready for new challenges—even if she is not sure what the future holds.

SELF-ASSESSMENT

Melissa, Zayid, and Jasmine are each at a pivotal point in their teaching careers. How will they get to the next level? Who will help them get there? If they were to do a self-assessment identifying their strengths and challenges, it might look like table 2.1.

Now it's time for you to create a snapshot of where you are (table 2.2) using the template in exhibit 2.1 at the end of the chapter. Think about your strengths and the challenges you face given your particular teaching situation.

How did you do? Would you be willing to share your snapshot with people you respect and get their feedback? If so, go for it.

TABLE 2.1 **Snapshots of our three archetypal teachers**

Teacher	Strengths	Goals
TechnoWhy? Melissa—high school history teacher with twenty-one years' experience	• Is passionate and knowledgeable in her subject area and interested in all of the humanities • Has many years of teaching and solid reputation within the school community • Enjoys personal challenges, especially with competitive swimming and photography	• To find the courage to try new teaching strategies; to take risks in her teaching • To seek out edtech courses and/or free webinars that will open her eyes to the potential of new tools to improve her practice (for all students, including those who are advanced and hearing impaired) • To connect with edtech enthusiasts right in her high school and community for inspiration and mentoring/coaching
TechnoOK Zayid—middle school English teacher with nine years' experience	• Finds it second nature to get his students up and running with digital tools • Enjoys the novelty and excitement of trying out new teaching strategies • Knows how to motivate adolescents who have "checked out" of academics	• To figure out how to go deeper; to use edtech in ways that have greater impact on student learning, particularly with regard to comprehension, vocabulary, and writing • To develop long-range strategies for technology integration • To use new tools to adapt instruction for all one hundred fifty of his students; to provide special adaptations for ELLs/EALs
TechnoYes! Jasmine—fourth-grade teacher (all subject areas) with five years' experience	• Has boundless energy and enthusiasm for TechnoTeaching • Is curious about the affordances of digital tools and is always thinking of ways to use them creatively • Has the talent and temperament required to be a school leader	• To develop a cohesive plan for using new tools in all subject areas every day/week/month in the school year • To be inspired by other educators well beyond her school walls • To use technology in ways that will help all of her students, including those with additional educational needs (AEN, in U.K. terminology); specifically teaching students with behavioral issues and more actively engaging their parents • To be an effective TechnoTeacher leader in her immediate world and at the national level

TABLE 2.2   **Snapshot of you as a TechnoTeacher**

You	Strengths	Goals
Teacher of:	• Am knowledgeable and passionate about . . .	• To find the courage to . . .
Number of students:	• Can offer . . .	• To seek out edtech courses and/or free webinars focused on . . .
Number of years of teaching experience:	• Enjoy . . .	• To use technology in ways that help students with these individual needs:

ASSESSING SKILLS & TOOLS, CONTENT, AND MINDSET

Now let's go deeper into our practice and contemplate Skills & Tools, Content, and Mindset. Our experiences have shown over and over again that teachers who regularly take stock of their practice and plan ahead have greater impact on student learning than those who wing it. Yet, often when we suggest the idea of taking stock to teachers, they resist, seeing it as an extra burden. They might shrug and say, "I'd like to take stock, but there's no way I can find time," or, "My school doesn't have enough resources for me to go down this edtech path. It's all I can do to schedule my class for the computer lab twice a month." Administrators might say, "Most of my teachers feel stretched as it is. I'm not willing to ask them to add something else to their list." We hear you. And we have been there ourselves, working in underresourced communities that lack even the most basic supplies like crayons and construction paper, let alone state-of-the-art equipment.[1] But think how eye-opening it would be if a year from now you had a record of where you were when you began your Techno-Teaching journey. Then you could measure how far you have come.

In this spirit, we have provided a "space" for you to begin reflecting, assessing, and planning for your own DIY TechnoTeaching Self-Assessment Plan (see exhibit 2.1 at the end of this chapter). It is one that you may want to share with your principal (line manager). You may choose to get started right away, or you may prefer to do your self-assessment after reading this entire book. It's your choice. We know that, just like the students in our classrooms, the teachers in the staff room all learn differently.

If you prefer a more holistic approach, you should continue to read the book, and then do the practical work once you have your head around the concept of being a TechnoTeacher. If however, you prefer to work in a methodical way— one step at a time—this may be the time for you to reflect on your own practice.

Here are a few ideas to get you started.

1. Team up with your curriculum coordinator, technology specialist, and/ or fellow teachers. Invite them to meet in your classroom, or in the

teacher's lounge. Arrange to have coffee, tea, and treats on hand. (Soul searching always makes us crave snacks.)

2. Agree to be honest. To be bold. To write down your ideas (on paper or digitally) as a commitment to yourself. Sometimes just stating your goals in front of others will strengthen your resolve.

3. Work through the set of questions we have provided in the Self-Assessment Plan to get a handle on where you are on the technology integration continuum. Take into account your particular Skills & Tools, Content, and Mindset. Think about the wider world beyond you as a resource. Include the tools you have access to—your classroom design and the "neutral," bookable spaces in your building that you can schedule in advance. You want to ensure that you have the tools and the space to help support you in this adventure. Then decide on your TechnoTeaching goals and your plan for accomplishing them.

4. Agree that you will not try to be perfect. Nobody is. Settle on a few short-term and one or two long-range goals that will help you walk that fine line between developing the talents you already have and stretching yourself in new directions. (Hold on to these goals so we can cycle back to them in chapter 8 when you reflect on the past year.)

5. Even though we lean toward starry-eyed optimism, we realize that not all of your peers will be thrilled to learn that you are retooling your practice. How will you respond to naysayers, particularly teachers who still hope edtech will go away even knowing that it's here to stay? Any chance you could persuade them to join forces with you and your teammates? Or, if you are an administrator, how can you set a positive, collegial tone in your district that supports these types of professional development efforts? No matter what, don't let the critics rain on your parade.

6. Taking your professional development seriously is part of taking yourself seriously. Own it! Create a folder (paper or digital) to keep track of your progress. Include your self-assessments and goals and label the folder "On the Way to Awesome." You might find that table 2.2

and exhibit 2.1 help you get started. Revisit your folder often and add the techniques and strategies you are learning about.

7. Create another folder and label it "Inspiration." Use it to keep track of all the TechnoTeaching ideas you come across related to your goals in exhibit 2.1 and as you continue on this journey.

In the following chapters, we will guide you through planning, creating, resourcing, and sharing a yearlong plan that *will* help you improve your teaching practice by integrating digital tools in dynamic ways you have yet to imagine.

EXHIBIT 2.1   **Do It Yourself TechnoTeaching Self-Assessment Plan**

Teacher(s) _____   Date _____

Meet with your colleagues and respond honestly and courageously to the following questions about Skills & Tools, Content, and Mindset.

1. SKILLS & TOOLS. *How well do you use a variety of edtech and other digital tools to learn new ones with ease? How well do you access resources and support systems that can help students learn these skills and acquire the necessary tools?*

Self-assessment for Skills & Tools	Responses	How can I reach the next level as a TechnoTeacher? (See prompts below)
What are my strengths?		Take courses; watch YouTube videos designed for educators (e.g., TED Talks for Educators); observe other teachers in action.
In general, how do I want to update my practice?		Better integrate digital tools, reflection, and knowledge of standards.
Which skills will give me the biggest payoff when it comes to TechnoTeaching and student learning?		Set up a blog; create a class website.
What are my students' strengths when it comes to using new tools?		Develop Internet research skills; understand how to evaluate sources for authenticity.
How can we share our skill sets with others in the school and beyond?		Give lunchtime presentations; host professional development events in my school and beyond.

EXHIBIT 2.1 *(continued)*   **Do It Yourself TechnoTeaching Self-Assessment Plan**

Teacher(s) _____   Date _____

2. CONTENT. *How well do you integrate technology in a deliberate manner to engage students in the curriculum in ways that would not otherwise be possible? How well do you meet the needs of all learners?*

Self-assessment for Content	Responses	How can I reach the next level as a TechnoTeacher? (See prompts below)
In which curricular units have I been most successful in integrating new tools?		Teach _____ using _____ to help students really learn the content.
How can I build on this success (above) and infuse other curricular units with digital tools?		Add a digital timeline to a history unit; publish student poetry.
What types of digital tools would enhance project-based learning?		Incorporate iPad apps; use tablets for note taking; find a way to project digital presentations.
How can I get my hands on these tools and learn how to use them?		Ask tech specialists for help; partner with local businesses; write a mini-grant.
How can I use digital tools to differentiate my curriculum to meet the needs of all students?		Use software for English language learners; integrate adaptive technologies for students with individual needs.
What digital tools can my students use to communicate what they have learned?		Use presentation software, infograms, and/or podcasts; post on a class website.
How can I use digital tools to help assess my students' understanding of a curricular unit?		Use online formative evaluation tools.

EXHIBIT 2.1 *(continued)*   **Do It Yourself TechnoTeaching Self-Assessment Plan**

Teacher(s) _____   Date _____

3. MINDSET. *To what extent do you embrace the use of new technology? How willing are you to take risks and engage in continuous learning and reflection in order to ensure that students are well prepared to assume their role as global citizens?*

Self-assessment for Mindset	Responses	How can I reach the next level as a TechnoTeacher? (See prompts below)
What can students teach me? What can they teach their peers?		Be willing to (sometimes) give up the expert role; give students many opportunities to explore the capabilities of various edtech tools.
Do students associate my lessons with contemporary forms of writing and reading and communicating? If so, why? If not, how can I get in step with the times?		Use digital tools to help improve my literacy program; learn from leading innovators; mentor others if literacy instruction is one of my strengths.
Where can I find inspiration for edtech integration? What models can I seek out to inspire me?		Observe teachers in my community in action; attend a great edtech conference.
How can students access digital tools outside of my lessons?		Develop relationships with libraries, universities, and community centers.
How can I become a positive force of change within my school system and beyond?		Be open to learning new things; share what I've learned; lead the way with global citizenship.
How can I become more of an edtech leader?		Find encouragement; overcome shyness; reach out to others beyond my immediate environment; lead professional development sessions.

CHAPTER 3

Jumping In

The Stellar Unit

Now that you have met our three TechnoTeachers and stepped back to reflect on your own practice, we will show you how to jump-start your plan for integrating technology into your classroom. The next step in becoming a TechnoTeacher is to design at least one special, media-rich unit based on your curriculum and the strengths you identified in the previous chapter. We call each of these carefully crafted units of study a *Stellar Unit*.

The idea is this: building a repertoire of Stellar Units, at your own pace, over the course of several months will represent several giant steps on your way to becoming a TechnoTeacher. Having this repertoire will not only give you confidence, it will also strengthen and enliven your teaching on several different levels.

In this chapter we offer vignettes of our three archetypal teachers in action, trying out their Stellar Units for the first time. Not everything goes smoothly. But lessons are learned as things go awry. We hope you will recognize something of yourselves as you read each scenario. But first, let's go over the basics of identifying and designing a Stellar Unit.

WHAT IS A STELLAR UNIT?

What is the very best curricular unit you teach? The one you look forward to teaching every year? If you are a new teacher, it might be a unit you learned about in your student days. Or it might be a subject you cotaught as part of your teacher training. Then, over time, you became passionate about it. Veteran teacher or beginner—you are at your all-time best when teaching this unit. This passion serves as the impetus for designing your very particular, idiosyncratic Stellar Unit.

This is your Stellar Unit. "Finding that passion," says Sir Ken Robinson, "is an inherently personal process . . . [I]t's important to remember that teaching is not a process of transmission—it is an art form." And the more you develop your art form, the more your lessons become personalized.[1]

For the new teacher out there, trust us. You will want to have one signature piece that will be your jumping-off point for the rest of your career. We will show you how to develop one, based on our experiences with teaching technology-rich units (in Nicole's case) and teaching Language and Literacy graduate students how to infuse their curriculum with digital media (in Julie's case).

DESIGNING YOUR STELLAR UNIT

To illustrate the idea of a Stellar Unit, we will show how each of our fictitious teachers conceptualizes a medium-term teaching plan (i.e., five to seven weeks). Integral to the process are the three elements we discussed previously and illustrated in figure 1.1: Skills & Tools, Content, and Mindset. *Skills & Tools* refers to the twenty-first-century skills the TechnoTeachers are already good at, or are willing to learn. The tools include whatever computers and gadgets teachers can get their hands on—digital cameras, photo editing software, the Internet—to integrate into their lessons.

The element of Content requires the teachers to integrate technology in a deliberate manner to engage students in the curriculum in ways that would be difficult otherwise (e.g., exchanging letters with peers halfway around the world). Each TechnoTeacher's content will also address the needs of different groups of students and their varying ability levels.

The Mindset the TechnoTeacher brings to a project will have a strong impact on his or her willingness to venture into new terrain, embrace new tools, take risks, and engage in continuous learning. Mindset also is a key factor in how well the three TechnoTeachers prepare their students to take on the role of global citizens.

When it is time for you to design your Stellar Unit, we recommend that you begin with a curricular unit that you are particularly comfortable with. We also suggest that you use tools that you have used before and which are right in your cupboard, as our TechnoTeachers do. We ask you to stretch a bit, using your Stellar Unit as a jumping-off point for trying out a website or medium you have been meaning to experiment with.

Although your goals and objectives may be quite different from those of our TechnoTeachers, their experiences (including missteps and small victories) will shed light on how to design your own Stellar Unit. Also, be sure to review all of your "think work" from chapter 2 (your snapshot of you as a TechnoTeacher, and your DIY Self-Assessment Plan). Your notes will help organize your thinking for your first Stellar Unit, and ultimately your blueprint for the year—but more on that in chapter 4.

Before we jump in, we would like to say a word to U.S. teachers about the Common Core State Standards (CCSS). We can't help being struck by the fact that every teacher is supposed to be teaching literacy skills in every subject area. Also, integrating edtech is no longer simply optional. As you can see in box 3.1, children as young as kindergarteners are expected to be able to use technology and digital media creatively and effectively on the way to becoming "college and career ready in reading, writing, speaking, listening, & language."[2] We will show you examples, through our fictitious teachers, of how you can meet the CCSS goals using technology in creative and dynamic ways.

> ### BOX 3.1   CCSS technology goals
>
> According to the Common Core State Standards goals for technology: "Students employ technology thoughtfully to enhance their reading, writing, speaking, listening, and language use. They tailor their searches online to acquire useful information efficiently, and they integrate what they learn using technology with what they learn offline. They are familiar with the strengths and limitations of various technological tools and mediums and can select and use those best suited to their communication goals."[3]

STELLAR UNITS AND OUR TECHNOTEACHERS: THREE SCENARIOS

Let's look over the shoulders of Melissa, Zayid, and Jasmine as they teach their first Stellar Unit of the year. As you read their journeys, consider our advice and imagine how you would approach these units and what you can learn from each one. (Also, check out their completed Stellar Unit outlines at the end of this chapter.)

We will incorporate our three TechnoTeaching elements—Skills & Tools, Content, and Mindset—into the vignettes so you can track their progress as TechnoTeachers. We will also offer our own advice to help individualize support for each one. We realize that this advice will not help everyone, but we will "speak" to each TechnoTeacher as we would to any of our mentees. It might also be fun to consider what advice you would give our TechnoTeachers!

We will start with Melissa, our TechnoWhy? teacher, as she is the least confident in terms of her Skills & Tools and Mindset. Content is not so much of an issue here, as she is exceptionally strong in her subject matter.

TechnoWhy? Melissa: Rhode Island History in Photographs and Essays

Melissa knew exactly what wanted to teach as her Stellar Unit: Rhode Island history, hands down. Her interest in this seaside resort never wanes. While most tourists head for the mansions built by the Vanderbilts and other wealthy industrialists, Melissa heads for the historic district—the three-hundred-year-old structures that lend the town the full weight of history amid all the yachts, wealthy heiresses, and craggy shorelines.

Melissa has been refining her Rhode Island history unit for several years. She relies on a history textbook and primary source materials (such as sea captains' journals, old maps, and letters) alongside paintings from the era and historical novels. Since she is confident in her knowledge of the content, she has decided that Skills & Tools and Mindset are the areas in which she wants to challenge herself the most. Ultimately, she would like to become comfortable with using technology in ways that allow her students to take ownership. She will begin by asking them to make choices about how *they* want to assimilate content knowledge. Once they become experts in their subject area, she will encourage them to create new types of products, like a class blog, rather than writing the old-fashioned book reports she used to assign.

A new staff developer, Mimi, urges Melissa to infuse her favorite unit with digital tools to make it "twenty-first-century-appropriate." The very phrase strikes fear in Melissa's heart. She has a flashback to the unit that went awry due to a phantom-like Internet connection. Students became impatient and borderline rowdy when the Internet went down. Melissa felt as though the rug had been pulled out from under her feet. She would never let that happen again, Mimi or no Mimi.

Now to launch her first Stellar Unit . . .

Jules advises   You will see how all three of our TechnoTeachers were already skilled in project-based learning *and the sort of small-group work that is part and parcel of this approach. Project-based learning is not new. It dates back over one hundred years to John Dewey and his ideas about the Progressive movement in education. As a social reformer, Dewey urged educators to move away from rote learning and instead learn pragmatic skills in the community. He believed relevance to students' lives should be at the forefront of teachers' goals. And with project-based learning comes group work, which benefits learners in multiple ways.*

Group work allows the teacher to create homogeneous groups (to focus on learning a particular skill) and heterogeneous groups (to maximize peer learning and bring diverse skill sets to the forefront). There's a time and a place for each—and they can be fluid within a unit of study, with children assigned to different groups for Skills & Tools, writing, research, and so on. You might also have students create their own interest groups.

In Melissa's case, groups will be largely heterogeneous. Besides promoting learning and peer teaching, the groups will also be important for classroom management. With 175 students to teach in a given day, Melissa needs to put structures in place to help her focus her instruction and have students work together productively. Later in this chapter, you will see how Zayid and Jasmine group their students and how they keep track of their progress.

Week 1: Launch the Stellar Unit

I don't have to climb Mt. Everest in the first day, right? Small, bite-sized steps—isn't that what Mimi said? Melissa hears these words in her mind as she swims her morning laps. *And photography is my thing, right? Along with history? I also know how to group students for project-based learning. So I should be good at this. But even the best-laid plans . . .* Melissa is pleased that her daughter, Daisy, came to dinner last night. It gave them the chance to chat about Mimi's point of view in advance.

Daisy gave Melissa lots of great advice. Melissa smiles as she remembers how thrilled she was to be able to ask questions, in and with confidence—to have a secret project to share with her daughter. Melissa chuckles to herself, feeling very proud that Daisy is now able to teach her a few things about planning a lesson with technology. Namely, Daisy said, *"Give it a go, take some risks, and ask, what's the worst that can happen?"*

Melissa hopes she can be as fearless as the daughter she raised. She looks at her snapshot and decides to bring into play her passion for photography to help students learn how to frame an interesting shot (using light/dark and interesting angles), edit it using digital software, and then upload it online as a class blog. The more she thinks about it, the more she decides that this type of teaching will result in more dynamic student projects than the static reports she used to assign, which were read by an audience of only one (i.e., her!).

An hour later, Melissa stands before her first-period class. "Remember when I told you we had a special unit coming up? Your assignments will be to work in groups to create a photo essay on Rhode Island history to publish online. We'll begin by capturing Newport in photographs—starting with the Revolutionary War–era structures—houses, churches, and statues in the colonial part of town. I want you to choose interesting angles and think about the role of light and shadows in your work."

Melissa hands out digital cameras, one per small group of students. "I think you'll discover that recording history, using cameras, sharpens your senses. You'll begin to see things in a new way. And you will become the observers and recorders of history. I want you to consider what it was like to have been one of the first people to see these buildings, or even to have been one of their builders. What do the buildings say to you?

"We need sharp eyes and a sense of adventure. We need to be real-time detectives, because as you know—come on, let's hear it—*history is everywhere.*" Students have heard Melissa say this so often, they recite it along with her. They may even believe it.

"Okay, we need teams—reporters, photographers, researchers. Who knows how to use desktop publishing tools?" Hands shoot up around the room. "Great. I have had a quick tutorial on this. But I realize many of you are experts. Let's get started."

By the end of the class period, students have sorted themselves into groups and taken on various roles according to their interests. Melissa makes sure each group is heterogeneous, with eight advanced students spread out rather than clustered together.

Tomorrow Melissa will meet with advanced students about using their project as a way to do a deep dive into history. They will act as the directors of the groups, asking questions and guiding their groups—as a small army of mini–student teachers. Will their project involve graphic design? Or digging through primary source materials (on the Library of Congress's website, for example)? How will they suggest using technology?

Nic advises   With advanced students, there are two ways you can direct them. You can have them focus on higher-order thinking skills (analysis, synthesis, evaluation, application, and justifying answers). Or you can get them to develop their multimedia skills (by designing web pages or blogs, looking at conventions of genre, or working as a team on a production, for example).

If active engagement in learning is your main goal, the second option might be a good way to go, especially if you are unsure about your own multimedia skills.

For this unit, the more gifted students in Melissa's class may decide to create a podcast with the photographs, rather like a "tour" of the town. Or they could create a visual essay, via a blog, with Vimeo video footage (sourced) combined with images of their own work. They might also create a documentary or a website, using a map of the area with interactive links to key historical sites.

You may find some students are ready to take on the role of teacher. This is okay. You can learn along with them. Then, the next time you teach this unit, you will be even more ready to take the lead.

If you wish to stretch students' thinking skills, you may be able to find a combination of the multimedia ideas and the processes of evaluation or analysis. You can use a podcast with evidence cited, for example, or a documentary with primary and secondary interviews, which they can evaluate for authenticity.

It will also be important to develop a plan to ensure that students with additional educational needs are provided with differentiated instruction. To personalize the learning experience for hearing impaired students, for example, you could ask them to work with a group and offer advice on how to make the text more helpful for hearing impaired audiences (e.g., by including subtitles, brainstorming how to use radio or hearing aids in innovative ways, or using sound in different ways—or not at all). You can ask these students to take the lead on this aspect of the project, as they will know what the audience (they themselves!) would appreciate the most.

It would also be a good idea to look at resources from museums for the hearing impaired or contact a national charity or organization to be one step ahead here.

In any case, any or all of these activities will benefit students academically and technologically; they will also help you close the gap on some of your TechnoTeacher challenges.

Week 1 (continued): Take students on a Newport field trip

The die is cast. I'm about to take six different groups of adolescents—all of my classes—to the old section of Newport to take photographs. And it looks like rain. I am either brilliant or crazy.

Melissa and three parent volunteers chaperone each group of students to the historic sites they've been assigned to focus upon, from the Quaker Meeting House to Queen Anne Square. After some initial goofing off, students shift into a more serious mode. They get so immersed by taking pictures that Melissa has to corral them into the school vans when class is over. *Phew, no disasters yet.*

Week 2: Meet with teams of students

Melissa meets with each team for fifteen-minute debriefing sessions. Each team presents what they have so far—their notes, photographs, and sketches. Melissa uses a conference form for note taking (see exhibit 3.1 at the end of this chapter), which is part of the tech toolkit Mimi and Daisy helped her create.

Melissa is a tough critic. She doesn't let anyone get by with glib answers. Instead she pushes students to work harder, dig deeper, and synthesize what they've discovered from reading multiple sources.

She is surprised to learn that her students already know how to use photo editing tools and get to work right away. *Ha! Here I thought I had to get up to speed on all these tools—to be the absolute expert—only to discover that my students are ten steps ahead of me. I will try really hard to have a Zen-like attitude about giving up the role of expert . . . Deep breaths.*

Week 3: Have students conduct research

Melissa watches as three student reporters huddle at a computer working on a visual essay about local history, which they will eventually post to the classroom blog. Today they search for background information. They locate the PBS LearningMedia website, which offers videos, games, and images on all kinds of subjects.[4]

Melissa observes two other students, Josh and Olivia, searching the LearningMedia site. *Very cool. Their research skills are coming along. Their group should be in good shape when it's time to present their visual essay and post it to the website.*

Week 3 (continued): Have groups work on a "tour of the town" podcast and a visual essay, via a blog

Melissa watches as Josh posts several photos of Newport's Truro Synagogue on the corkboard that covers an entire wall of the classroom. He is trying to decide which ones best illustrate his group's podcast (which will be "a tour of the town") about the early settlers and religious freedom.

He stands back and studies work the other groups have tacked up: photos of interview subjects, a timeline with events and photos taped to it, biographies of sea captains and their families alongside photos of their grand homes. He also studies the rough outlines posted by the visual essay group—which they keep rearranging every time inspiration strikes.

Today is the day. Students will write about the most remarkable things they've learned for a visual essay (for the blog), which will help them tap into the deep currents of American history. What have they found out about the Vikings who supposedly settled Newport in the early days (lots of lore but no evidence)? Colonial architecture? The King Charles Charter of 1663, the first such legislation for freedom of religion and separation of church and state?

A student asks Melissa if she can also post tips on using photo editing, illustration, and desktop publishing tools. "Great idea," Melissa says. "Other students will appreciate it, as will I! And, of course, be sure to document everything."

Week 4: Perform a quick, formative evaluation

Melissa jots down the URL for a quiz she has created on the board as two students distribute iPads from a mobile cart.

"Go to this website to take a pop quiz. This is just a quick check to help us gauge how you're doing. I will still assign three essay questions at the end of the unit for a more in-depth evaluation of your work."

Breathe in. Breathe out. She thought students might balk at this pop quiz, but instead they got right to it. "If you're working on a computer, type in the URL that's on the board and go from there."

Melissa was initially against giving a digital pop quiz even though she's a believer in formative evaluations. Once she realized how easy it is to create and score a quiz, and how useful it is to have a quick snapshot of what students are learning about history, she changed her mind. She entered the quiz questions she used to hand out to students on paper. And nothing crashed.

Today's quiz helps Melissa evaluate whether students have any misconceptions about the material. If they do, she will meet with them in small groups, and organize a couple of peer teaching sessions. *How cool am I? Not very. But I am beginning to find my way.*

Week 5: Have students present and evaluate one another's work

Melissa asks the two groups to take turns presenting their projects. The first group presents its podcast, "A Tour of the Town," which includes photos and a timeline. The second group shows their visual essay. They have found some public domain clips that they can use, and have supplemented them with video clips of their own. It is a work in progress, not ready to be posted to the blog.

Melissa sets the tone for how the two teams should critique each other's work. She models how to be diplomatic yet also offer strategies to help others improve their work.

Jules advises When it comes to peer editing, you may find that critiquing one another's writing can be a rich learning experience for students—both for those who are giving constructive criticism and those who are receiving it. But things can easily go awry if students are not respectful of one another. Remind your students about the type of feedback that is most helpful for the writer—including focusing on the questions the writer asks about his or her work.

Engage students in role-playing scenarios where they can take turns modeling how to give positive yet constructive feedback. Make these sessions part of your writers' workshops throughout the school year. How can you keep track of who is working on what, and which students you should schedule first for one-on-one conferences with you? Nancie Atwell, a well-respected expert on student writing (and one of my idols, in fact), recommends that you spend the first few *minutes of your writers' workshop on "Status of the Class," so students can report what they're planning to work on that day. Having students describe their work speaks volumes about their progress, both immediately and over time.[5]*

As a TechnoTeacher, you can add digital writing Skills & Tools to the equation—either online (using the Internet or an intranet) or offline (saving to computer desktops or storage areas). Both will make the composing and editing process more fun—and efficient— than simple writing with pen and paper.

Begin by having students create their outlines and first drafts using word processing tools. Take advantage of spell check and thesaurus resources along with software that makes it easy to create graphic organizers for prewriting activities.

Show students how to create digital folders to help organize their drafts. For more advanced learners, try introducing them to peer editing tools (through Google Docs, for example). You can also show students with individual needs how to enlarge text and access "read aloud" features. In addition, you can look into software that supports process writing, such as Write: Outloud, which offers a multisensory approach (including a talking spell checker), or try Co:Writer, which attempts to anticipate the next word in a sentence and allows users to select a word by clicking.[6] Also see Dragon Dictate, which allows students with special needs to bypass the keyboard altogether.

If you haven't already made the transition to integrating digital tools into your writing program, find out what resources your school has and who can help you get started.

A few days ago, Melissa panicked over whether she could deal with the in-class presentations. She decided to recruit the tech coordinator, who agreed to be on standby. It turned out she needed his help only once or twice, but know-ing that she *could* get help the minute she needed it set her mind at ease.

To conclude the Rhode Island history unit, Melissa plans to have students create assessment portfolios, culling their best work. These portfolios will become the backbone of her assessment plan for students. Although students have created digital content, Melissa doesn't feel ready to commit to digital online portfolios. She is still nervous about the lack of control of having them "out there" in cyberspace. Maybe next year, with tech support from Mimi. For now Melissa gives herself a pat on the back for having aligned her teaching with the CCSS, as summarized in box 3.2.

Week 6: Share students' work with the community

The walls of the school's entryway are lined with "Rhode Island History Night" posters. Families help themselves to a student-designed program and take a seat in the auditorium. A student hangs a Dorothea Lange quotation in the entryway: "The camera is an instrument that teaches people how to see with-out a camera."

After a few introductory remarks, Melissa hands over the microphone to the boy and girl who act as MCs for tonight's presentations. Students will share

---

BOX 3.2 Aligning the Stellar Unit to CCSS

Melissa's Stellar Unit aligns with the Common Core State Standards in the following ways (in addition to technology goals):

- Building knowledge through content-rich nonfiction and informational texts
- Reading and writing grounded in evidence from text
- Engaging in regular practice with complex text and its academic vocabulary
- Including related goals like discussion and written compositions in both fiction and nonfiction text genres

their podcasts with the audience against a backdrop of their photographs. The second half of the presentation will involve having students present their visual essays and invite questions and comments from the audience.

Five minutes in, a boy forgets his line. Melissa's stomach clenches. He recovers quickly and the show is under way. The tech coordinator has begun filming the two presentations. When she's further along the TechnoTeaching curve, Melissa might be open to learning how to edit the videos and post them to the school website, if she can get the tech support she needs.

Melissa's first Stellar Unit has taught her a bit about humility. *Since I'm not up to speed on the technical side, something could go horribly wrong. But it won't be the end of the world. Right? Right. As Daisy said, what it comes down to is this: whatever mistakes are made tonight will only make you and your students stronger in the end—better than having lost your nerve.*

Melissa feels her blood rising up her neck, her face getting red. She closes her eyes and fans herself with a program.

Later, after the applause has died down, after families have disappeared into the chilly autumn night, after the tech coordinator has given her two thumbs up, only then will Melissa allow herself to exhale.

Nic and Jules advise on Melissa's Stellar Unit

Visual essays, a blog, photo editing and desktop publishing software? How is it possible that a TechnoWhy? teacher like Melissa was able to navigate the rocky shoals of integrating all these tools for her first Stellar Unit?

(Nic) While Melissa's Rhode Island history unit may look overly ambitious on paper, in fact her students already knew how to use many of the tech tools that were important for their "tour of the town" and visual essay (using Vimeo). These are students who grew up narrating their presentations and using camcorders to film key

> *moments in their lives without thinking twice. They have taught her in this instance.*
>
> *(Jules) The reason this Stellar Unit was manageable for Melissa is that she was courageous enough to change the way she'd always taught history. She also gave herself permission to learn alongside her students. Although she had only a cursory knowledge of desktop publishing tools, she decided not to wait until she was completely proficient.*
>
> *Forging ahead on this project, without being 100 percent sure of herself, wasn't easy for Melissa. She had a few missteps along the way. But the upside was that students already knew so much about using new tools that she was able to tap into this knowledge base. Also, a few colleagues (and Daisy) were there with a life raft when she needed one.*
>
> *Now that she knows what she and her students are capable of, there's no turning back.*

TechnoOK Zayid: Digital Storytelling

Zayid heads for his home office, hoping his sons will fall asleep without asking him for yet more stories or to check for crocodiles under the bed. He fires up his laptop and clicks on a folder for one of his English classes. Within that folder he has organized student work according to which group they're working in—three in all.

Zayid has had students work on outlining their narrative structure for their digital stories. Tonight he plans to review their work so far. His hunch is that some groups have a clearly defined plot with built-in action and drama (featuring zombies, aliens, and time travelers?), while others need a bit more instruction.

Tomorrow Zayid will set up conferences, starting with the groups who need help. He'll even try out the conference sheet that will supposedly help him document student progress. But for now, he uses the "add comment" feature of his word processing software to give feedback.

Zayid has always looked forward to teaching narrative plot structure in his digital storytelling unit. He swears by the effectiveness of plot structure as a way to help students find their voices as writers. This year he will integrate more media into his unit. No more storyboards scrawled on paper. No more of his red-inked comments in the margins. Today it's all about digital tablets and typing in digital suggestions. And while Zayid does like the solid feel of paper beneath his pen, digital devices make his job of mentoring one hundred fifty budding writers more efficient by an order of magnitude.

Digital storytelling is Zayid's Stellar Unit. Ted, the professional developer Zayid took a course with in July, encouraged Zayid to redesign this particular unit in light of how much he enjoys teaching it. Ted is a demon planner. He expects Zayid to plot out everything—all the particulars of showing students how to integrate art, video clips, photographs, narration, music, and even animation into their stories. Ted also encourages teachers to keep track of student work by using his conference form (see exhibit 3.1 at the end of this chapter).

Zayid thinks of himself as one to improvise, although he grudgingly filled out all the planning forms during the training. He's at odds with himself about how strictly he will adhere to them. *I have my own teaching style. And Ted has absolutely zero sense of adventure.*

Week 1: Launch the Stellar Unit

What is narrative? What makes a good story? What are some of your favorite stories, from both books and movies? What can we learn by analyzing them? Zayid walks around the room encouraging his students to be analytical thinkers.

The Hunger Games series inevitably comes up in each class. "What makes it so compelling?" Zayid asks. "What sorts of intrigues does the author create around good and evil? Bravery and cowardice? Competition?" Hands shoot up immediately.

Week 1 (continued): Ask students to brainstorm ideas for stories

Zayid has the "zombie" group meet at one of the big tables in the classroom. Per instructions, they designate a leader (a "director") and a note taker ("assistant") for the lesson. Zayid has considered the ELL/EAL students and their personal learning targets. The student who is currently better at writing English than speaking it is paired with a "buddy" to take notes. Another, who is a stronger speaker, takes on the role of director. The newest student in the class is paired with a learning support assistant/translator who is guiding her through the lesson, at a discrete distance.

Zayid circles the class, ensuring that the group dynamics are creative and productive. The "detective story" group meets nearby, while the "silent movie" group meets at a third table. The noise level soon goes from zero to sixty. Zayid spends time with each group. He hands out a checklist of what they need to include, such as generic conventions; a beginning, middle, and end; or three acts and a sense of the camerawork and sound. He makes sure that group leaders are allowing everyone to speak and keep on task, as a director would.

Then students work on a narrative and a tagline (a short, clever bit of advertising copy to attract viewers, as in "A story as big as life itself") to ensure they keep the audience in mind from the start. Some groups are more creative than others; Zayid bears this in mind for the following lessons to allow for extra support for several individuals.

Week 2: Have students create storyboards

"So there you have it," says Zayid. "Each narrative will have three acts. You will divide each act into two or three scenes—however many you need, but not *too* many. You'll need to develop a character arc for each of your main characters, and an ending in act three that pulls together all the story threads you've established in acts one and two, rather than a big twist."

Students work at computers using storyboard software to help them map out their narrative sequence. *Look how organized they are,* Zayid thinks. *Maybe there's something to all this planning. On the other hand, I wouldn't want it to keep them from being spontaneous. One of life's many conundrums.*

Zayid notices that the ELL/EALs are having a difficult time getting their peers to listen to their ideas. He has made a point of pairing his ELL/EAL students with English speakers, but this strategy is not working smoothly. He checks in with each group to reiterate the assignment and make sure the ELL/EALs get equal airtime. He notices that their story ideas are often rooted in tales from their cultures; this makes it hard for them to explain themselves quickly when everyone is vying for the spotlight. *Note to self: keep a careful eye on ELL/EALs to make sure their ideas are heard and respected. More directed teaching is needed here to give the groups the skills to do this independently.*

Week 3: Meet with groups of students

"I need to see the 'silent movie' group," Zayid says, grabbing a blank conference sheet. "Please bring your storyboards." He helps students nail down "the bones of the story" before they begin creating multimedia. (His former self would have let students take off on interesting tangents before they had their plot structure in place, which he learned to regret.) By the end of each class, everyone has posted their storyboards on the bulletin board.

Week 4: Have students create multimedia to add to storyboards

Yes! Finally. Zayid reserves time in the media lab on a day when the part-time media specialist is there. He asks if she'll help work with students. She agrees. Each group has made a list of the multimedia they plan to add to their narrative—from cartoons to manipulated photographs to fancy lettering. He's afraid that if students get stuck and have to wait to get unstuck, they'll lose their momentum. *Although plenty of kids are way more advanced than I am. Have I gone overboard in setting them loose with multimedia tools? Nah.*

Nic advises   Begin by determining the main learning outcome you are aiming for. Is it new media skills, or is it developing a narrative? Ensure that the focus is clearly on one or the other. Zayid *may find, for example, that students learn more about a piece of software or device in the process of securing a realistic story arc. Or he may discover that students have a fantastic idea for a character. They then decide to enhance their idea by doing something creative using blue screen or a piece of music as soundtrack.*

Either way, be sure not to let students spin too many plates, as they might end up dropping everything. You want them to be pleased with their final piece, but you have time limits, resource restrictions, and group dynamics to cope with. It's not as though you have a Hollywood budget and a year to help students produce their ideas. Keep their narratives focused and simple. Remember the aim of each project. You will end up with some fantastic work as a TechnoTeacher, work that will help lay your foundation for the rest of the school year.

Week 5: Have students integrate multimedia into their digital storyboards

Zayid thinks his students are ready to figure out how to integrate multimedia into their storylines. One team works with digital photographs. Another creates an animation. A third records a soundtrack on an iPad. Several students get together to film a short scene. The classroom looks like mayhem, but is in fact very organized and productive.

Zayid can't shake the nagging sensation that he might have taken on too much for one project. Next time, he might limit the media options for digital storytelling to photographs and soundtracks. He can add more options as the year progresses. A more gradual approach would give students more time to develop their expertise. They could focus more easily. *I might focus more easily!*

Week 6: Ask students to critique one another's work

Through student presentations, Zayid discovers that some projects have veered off-course, with the multimedia components edging out the narrative flow. A few problems could have been nipped in the bud at conferences. Except that Zayid admits that he has let some of the group meetings slip by. He creates a new conference schedule immediately and posts it on the whiteboard.

Week 6 (continued): Perform formative evaluation focused on narrative

"Leave time at the end of today's class to answer a few questions about narrative structure and story arcs on Socrative," says Zayid. "You'll see the Socrative app on your iPad. Click on it and then answer the short quiz. That way, I can tell who understands story structure and who needs a quick review."

After class, Zayid does a quick runthrough of student data. This is the first time he has used an online formative evaluation tool. Although the class performed much as he had expected, he discovers that a few students, several of them ELL/EALs, need more practice with characterization and plot development.

This week or next, Zayid will ask students to collect their best pieces as the first entry into this year's assessment portfolios. Similar to Melissa, Zayid doesn't feel he has the bandwidth right now to go 100 percent digital in collecting and assessing student work. Maybe next year.

Nic advises Be creative and inspired by technology, but make sure you are developing students' learning skills. For example, when teaching The Outsiders a few years ago, I had my students create Facebook pages for the characters. That way, they could use "status updates" to share quotations between the characters. The lower-attaining students especially loved this assignment. As the novel was used as an unseen text (a book that is not allowed in the exam), Facebook became a way for students to memorize key quotations offline, without actually accessing this social media platform.

Activities like this can help students appropriate new tools (per the ACOT stages listed in chapter 1).

Week 7: Hold the digital storytelling celebration

Students get ready for the digital storytelling celebration by transforming the gym into a narrative stage. Visitors will be invited to enter and watch one of three presentations, each one set up on a laptop. (Fortunately, Zayid's school was awarded a grant last year that allowed the IT specialist to purchase a dozen laptops to be shared across classrooms.)

Zayid's first step is to place the main projector screen at the front of the stage, and then use two mobile ones to project on either side of it (aiming one toward the ceiling and the other toward the floor). He places laptops around the tables by the front doors. His biggest challenge is to figure out what to do with the masses of power cables and extension cords, but tape and some well-placed chairs help camouflage the maze of wires and also help prevent people from tripping over them.

Never one to miss an opportunity to teach writing, Zayid has his students create advertisements for their narrative booths, which he hangs on flipcharts and mobile screens around the gym. He also has them write dramatic summaries of their stories and post them on the school website. When the students persuade Zayid to tweet an advertisement to the school community, he agrees, as long as they compose the message.

The night of the celebration goes smoothly, unless you count the number of times the wireless connection fades out. Or the fact that the principal frowns at all the snake-like wires on the floor, muttering something about a recipe for disaster. Or the two blown fuses.

Zayid's sons bounce from booth to booth. They are in awe of the "big kids" and beg to do something similar at home. Zayid feels the start of a tension headache and begins massaging his temples.

Maybe, even though I spent more time planning than usual, I did err on the ambitious side. But tonight will leave an indelible mark in students' minds. They may even begin to picture themselves as writers and multimedia developers some day.

Nic and Jules advise on Zayid's Stellar Unit

(Nic) Zayid may not have been as organized and methodical as he set out to be in teaching his digital storytelling unit (spontaneity sometimes trumped order), but he did try to narrow his focus. He limited the number of student groups to three. He managed to meet with groups several times, even though he intended to meet with them more often (a common struggle for teachers everywhere, we have noticed). And he worked on making the experience as educational and rewarding for his ELL/EAL students as possible.

(Jules) Zayid also learned that he needed to spend extra time with the ELL/EAL students to develop their listening and teamwork skills. He had not factored this in. It represented a positive shift for him to examine his teaching strategy rather than plow into the multimedia aspect. He enjoyed this challenge more than he cared to admit. It reminded him of why he had become a teacher in the first place.

All these factors contributed to the depth and richness of Zayid's Stellar Unit. They also got him into a TechnoTeacher frame of mind for the entire school year.

TechnoYes! Jasmine: International Keypals

The first teaching partner Jasmine ever had, Claudia, moved to Australia. After three years of coteaching fourth grade, Claudia announced that she and her husband were moving to a suburb of Sydney. "But don't worry. We'll stay in touch," Claudia said. "We can even do some sort of keypal exchange one of these days."

Today is the day, decides Jasmine, as she raids the school library, gathering all the atlases and books about Australia—studies on its rainforests; stories about kangaroos, wallabies, and koala bears. She also researches websites that will help her launch the student research projects she envisions.

Jasmine sends Claudia an e-mail message: "We're on. Let the exchange begin."

This keypal exchange will be Jasmine's first Stellar Unit. In creating an outline for each of six weeks, she will build on the penpal units she's taught before. But this time she'll go digital by meeting up with others online. (Be sure to see the resources in appendix B for ideas on connecting with another teacher for a keypal exchange if you don't have a colleague like Claudia waiting in the wings.)

There will be just one drawback. Students will not be able to "meet" via Skype given the vast number of time zones (fourteen!) separating Québec City and Sydney. But maybe children in each country will be able to capture their presentations using camcorders. Then they can learn how to edit them down to about two minutes each, and post them to their classroom website . . . *That's a possibility*, Jasmine thinks.

Nic advises   Given the time delay, I suggest combining two digital tools—first, using podcasts, so children can "speak" to one another, and second, creating blogs for written correspondence. Or you might decide to use the social media website Edmondo, where children from all over the world can learn more about one another.

An alternative idea is to have students introduce themselves by learning how to create and upload YouTube or Vimeo videos about their lives. If you decide to go this route, ask students to name their blogs (i.e., the blog needs to include the name of the individual or groups—for example, student121@classblog.TT). Then students will need to create links to all of the blogs (as described shortly in week 4). Although students will "own" the blogs, the teacher will oversee everything associated with them.

I recommend setting up one of these projects at the start of the Stellar Unit so you can get off to a smooth start. You'll be glad you took the time to figure everything out early on.

Week 1: Have students research Australia

The first stage is to have students learn everything they can about Australia, with a special focus on Sydney. (Claudia's students will work in parallel, studying Canada and Québec City.) Jasmine begins by introducing the jigsaw strategy. This technique involves organizing students into groups, according to their interests, to become experts on one of several subtopics: geography and climate, flora and fauna, and history and culture.

Students who sign up for geography and climate meet at a table in the corner. A boy volunteers to be the note taker as he and his classmates generate a list of questions they are curious about.

"Time to divide and conquer," Jasmine says, as she directs groups to the library, media center, or classroom computers. Then she circulates among teams. She engages students' higher-order thinking by having them evaluate the trustworthiness of the Internet resources they find. After forty-five minutes, Jasmine has students reconnect with their teammates and share what they learned today.

In a few weeks' time, each expert group will share more in-depth findings with the whole class. By the time the unit is finished, students will have a chance to take on both the expert and learner roles.[7]

Week 2: Ask students to write autobiographies and create self-portraits

Jasmine watches as a student mixes paint, trying to get the right color for her painting of herself playing the guitar. The boy working beside her also blends two colors. His self-portrait shows him riding a skateboard.

The students in both countries have decided that self-portraits would be more interesting to share with their keypals than digital photos. Jasmine and Claudia encourage students to upload these to the class intranet and create a podcast that they can e-mail to their new friends. *And our principals are hugely relieved by this decision*, thinks Jasmine. *Using art, not photos, reduces everyone's concerns about online predators.*

Similarly, Jasmine and Claudia keep a careful eye on their students' autobiographies. Even though they've warned their students not to include identifying information, the occasional street address or phone number slips in.

Jasmine confers with children in small groups so they can critique one another's autobiographies and self-portraits. Do their creations do a good job of capturing who they are? Do they give their keypals "hooks" that they can latch onto in their replies (e.g., hobbies, favorite music, movies, sports)?

Some of her students with behavioral issues have a hard time with the editing process. Two boys, for example, take Jasmine's constructive comments too personally. They act out by scribbling over other children's drafts and mixing the paints into an ugly, muddy brown color that nobody wants to use. This is a learning curve for Jasmine, as she thought they would all be excited and did not allow for low-level disruption. The boys are warned about their poor attitude toward learning and their peers, and are given a second chance to be involved. Jasmine moves the boys to her side and realizes that she will have to run a tight ship (for some more than others) in order for this to go well. Her backup plan is that these boys will compose the written assignment and be keypals with each other until their behavior improves.

Finally, the autobiographies and self-portraits are ready. Jasmine scans each one, makes folders for students, and posts them on the class intranet. She creates a backup copy on a USB pen in case there are any issues with the server. She can also use the USB copy if she decides to work on them at home.

Last, children make construction paper frames for their self-portraits and autobiographies and display them on the classroom bulletin board for Parents' Night. Jasmine takes photographs of everything so far and will eventually document the entire project and save files on her flash drive. One of these days, she hopes to present her work to teachers at an international conference.

Week 3: Assign keypals and have students e-mail their partners

Jasmine finishes writing names on the chalkboard and turns to her students. "Here's your partner, then. What would you like to know about him or her? Ready to send your compositions and art?"

They go to the school's tech lab and work at computers. Jasmine arranged beforehand for the tech coordinator to help students attach their scanned images (as jpegs) to their e-mail messages to their keypals. All the students already have e-mail accounts, so this is not an issue. She asks them to copy her on the e-mail so she can track everything. She thinks she might do a blog next time, as it would be easier to monitor.

The e-mail messages go out on a Tuesday morning. Jasmine checks the classroom e-mail account the next day. Nothing. But by Thursday morning, the inbox is filled with messages from Australia. Jasmine immediately reserves the lab for an hour that afternoon.

By the time children get to the computer lab, they are giddy with excitement. They can't wait to read the messages from their keypals and write back. To help frame their conversations, Jasmine and Claudia created a set of guidelines, shown in box 3.3.

Week 4: Have students e-mail their responses

Yes! Jasmine clicks on the messages she has received from other educators and tech coordinators, via an edtech social networking group she belongs to. Jasmine is used to being in the expert role. But this time, she has to admit, she was the one who needed advice. Ideas and suggestions poured in from all over the world. Some from certified "geeks" who live and breathe video production; others from well-meaning novices like herself.

BOX 3.3 Guidelines for keypal conversations

- Remember to respond to your keypal's autobiography and self-portrait. Ask questions or comment on some aspect of his or her artwork.
- Ask questions about the things in your keypal's culture that you're curious about (such as sports and what the school day is like there). Also be ready to ask a question about your research topic. If you are studying the rainforest, for example, you might ask your keypal if he or she has ever been to a rainforest. The idea is to get your keypal's firsthand perspective.
- Close your message with an interesting question or comment about yourself that your keypal will have fun answering.

"Hi Claudia. Here's how we might be able to share video clips," types Jasmine. "All we have to do is upload them to Vimeo or YouTube, or save them as QuickTime files and e-mail them. Another idea is to use Blogger and upload them, and put photographs in blogs. At least that's what a tech coordinator from Sweden suggested. What do you think?"

Jasmine pauses and raises an eyebrow. *I think I read that in my Techno-Teaching book!*

Week 4 (continued): Perform formative evaluation focused on behavior

"I have a better handle on tracking student learning than I do on behavior, I have to admit," Jasmine said to her team. "For this unit I'm planning to give ClassDojo, a tool to help with behavior management.[8] It's free. And they have an app you can use to help monitor both positive and negative behaviors. It might help me monitor three or four students in particular. I'm also thinking that the ClassDojo data might come in handy for parent conferences."

Week 5: Have students exchange video clips

Students are riveted to the short videos Jasmine projects onto the screen. They show their keypals presenting their research projects about Canada and sharing information about themselves and the world as they see it.

This is the second of two rounds of e-mail exchanges. Jasmine notices how valuable the video clips are in helping children in both countries get to know their counterparts in a more immediate way. Although some keypals in Sydney speak in accents that sound different to Canadian students' ears (and vice versa), slang (or kid culture) translates immediately. They are all interested in sports and popular culture. Some sing. Some show dance moves. Several Australians turn out to also be fans of *The Hunger Games* series.

If only I had signed up for that edtech conference in Montreal. This is really powerful stuff! Students have gained an awareness of Australia well beyond what they could learn through traditional research. And we've documented the entire project from start to finish. Maybe next year. Even if the mere thought of writing a proposal gives me hives.

Week 6: Share e-mail exchanges with parents

There is still a buzz about the keypals among Jasmine's students. She assigns them to work with their research groups and do the following:

- Connect the dots between what they studied in their research groups and what they learned from their keypals. Was there anything missing?
- Reflect on the funny, interesting, unexpected things they learned beyond the way their Australian peers greeted them with "G'day mate!" and referred to cookies as "biscuits." Some children said, "Don't worry, mate, she'll be right!" which means everything will be fine in the end.
- Then answer the big questions:
  - What did they learn about themselves from presenting themselves to others thousands of miles away?
  - What did they learn about their keypals in Sydney and how they view the world? What parts of their lives did they think were most important to share?

Once the students figure out the answers to these questions, they will share their ideas with peers across their grade level. Realizing that there is a parent event coming up, they ask Jasmine if they can create games for their families that involve the names of plants and animals and locating some of the places they have learned about on the map. Jasmine is all for it. After all, teaching is the best way to learn new material.

For assessment purposes, Jasmine used her professional development day to create a digital folder for each student that contains his or her e-mail exchanges. She has also archived the group projects about Australia. This will be the start of a yearlong e-portfolio assessment project. Again, next time she will use a classroom wiki and create a blog, which will streamline the whole process.

Nic and Jules advise on Jasmine's Stellar Unit

(Jules) Jasmine has stretched her students and herself immeasurably through her international keypals unit. Everyone involved has gained a more global worldview than would have been possible through more traditional methods.

(Nic) Yet even with Jasmine's advanced TechnoTeaching skills, there are a few areas that she would like to iron out next time. Her way of backing up and archiving student work was a bit complicated. If she (and students) had created a wiki and a blog from the start, they would have had a more streamlined way of saving and presenting student work. She also realizes that she needs to give more support to her additional educational needs (AEN) students—all did not go smoothly there. Nonetheless, she has caught the first edtech wave of the school year. It has been a terrific ride.

REFLECTING ON OUR TECHNOTEACHERS' STELLAR UNITS

These are just three examples of Stellar Units and how teachers brought them to life. In creating your first Stellar Unit, you might identify with TechnoWhy? Melissa and her near–panic attacks that everything digital will go awry. But she gathers her courage and plunges in anyway. Or you might identify with TechnoOK Zayid and his improvisational style, which can be both exciting and frustrating. Or, maybe you're like TechnoYes! Jasmine, who wants to be a teacher leader but is too busy actually teaching with technology to organize presentations for her district or national conferences.

Similarly, you might face some of the same challenges as our Techno-Teachers—challenging advanced students, learning more about hearing assistive technology (HAT), offering extra supports to ELL/EAL students and helping them shine, and working with students with AEN and/or behavioral issues.

Or you may feel that your level of sophistication as a TechnoTeacher is still evolving. You notice that you are courageous one day and timid the next; or that your students are unique, not at all like the ones described in this chapter.

That's fine! The idea is to design a Stellar Unit that aligns with your teaching philosophy and your students.

CREATING YOUR STELLAR UNIT

Your first Stellar Unit, to be launched in the beginning of the school year, can be broken down into a six-week outline. Use a copy of the template in table 3.1 to create a week-by-week outline of your Stellar Unit, adding details to each section.

Before you begin, ask yourself:

- What subject am I passionate about?
- What digital Skills & Tools do I want to try?
- What skills will *I* need to learn? By the same token, what skills will my *students* need to learn?
- How will I *integrate* the digital tools I'm considering into the curriculum?
- In ACOT terms (chapter 2), where does my Stellar Unit fit?
- How can I push my Mindset to be more of an innovator? More of a pioneer with edtech (using project-based learning and group work; taking a global perspective)?

Once you have considered questions like these, you are ready to create your first Stellar Unit outline. Be sure to refer back to it after each lesson if possible (or at least once a week) to reflect on how things are going before you teach your next class. (Even better, make this outline part of your teaching journal or notebook.) We are keen for this book to be as bespoke to you as it can be, regardless of your particular circumstances or how much experience you have in the field.

TABLE 3.1   **Stellar Unit outline: late September through October (six weeks)**

Weekly plan for Stellar Unit on:	Skills & Tools	Content	Mindset
Week 1			
Week 2			
Week 3			
Week 4			
Week 5			
Week 6			

What TechnoTeacher Skills & Tools might you need to take into account when you design your outline, based on where you are now? Table 3.2 offers some guidelines for you to consider as you hone your ideas according to where you are on the TechnoTeaching continuum (discussed in chapter 1). Also think about how you will not only learn from your colleagues, but also support their ideas and initiatives. As we have all learned, simply being a good listener and sharing what you've learned with your fellow teachers goes a long way toward building camaraderie and learning together.

ASSESSING YOUR STELLAR UNIT

Here are a few key questions for you to discuss with your colleagues.

1. How will you evaluate your student learning, both formally and informally, as part of the Stellar Unit?
2. How might your approach differ from your previous practice?

TABLE 3.2   **Tech goals to consider when designing your Stellar Unit**

Skills & Tools goals	Content goals	Mindset goals
Write in digital journals (perhaps double-entry).	Cover all skills required for subject/grade.	Bounce around ideas in the teachers' lounge.
Design classroom website and/or blog.	Differentiate instruction.	Participate in school-based professional development sessions.
Communicate via Skype and e-mail with peers in a different country.	Provide scaffolds for ELL/EAL students.	Show colleagues edtech strategies at lunch or after school.
Use tablets and apps for learning.	Collaborate with peers on curriculum.	Be an edtech leader within the school community.
Create multimedia publications.	Expand repertoire of teacher material (print and digital).	Contribute to global conversation and initiatives.
Record and post podcasts.	Participate in a cross-cultural exchange of some type.	Become a leader within the edtech community.

3. Which aspects of your Stellar Unit have you had success with? Which aspects were a little too pie-in-the-sky to be able to live up to?

When we work in schools and districts, teachers and administrators often ask us for simple, reliable measures for assessing students. They particularly want actionable data that will increase student learning. The type of actionable data they have in mind, such as teacher assessment or projected grades, can help school staff identify those students who are soaring ahead, those who need further reinforcement, and those who need one-on-one instruction.

From a more holistic perspective, educators also tell us that assessment practices in their schools are changing (or need to) in ways that align with the digital classroom. As high school social studies teacher Deborah McDevitt observed, "We're going to need to measure learning in different ways given what the iPad [and other tech tools] are bringing to the table . . . When you judge learning in traditional ways, you're not going to see huge jumps in multiple-choice tests because that's not what we're doing."[9] Exactly. We need to develop assessment tools that are closely aligned with the subject matter we teach.[10] The formative assessments mentioned in this chapter represent a small step in that direction.

We also need to think deeply about how to help our students succeed in twenty-first-century terms. As our definition of multimedia evolves, so too does our definition of what it means to be literate in today's world.

Helpful questions to ask yourself include:

- Are my students able to analyze and synthesize information from a variety of sources—TV, podcasts, movies, video, and the Internet?
- Can they suss out what is fact or opinion?
- Can they determine what is reliable information versus invented truths?
- Can they work with others to solve problems collaboratively and creatively?
- Are they skilled in sharing what they have learned with audiences—locally and perhaps even globally?

Today, these abilities are at the heart of teaching and learning—and can make being an educator more interesting and rewarding than at any other time in history.[11]

We suggest that you build your assessment plan into the outline for your first Stellar Unit right from the start, just as you would with a paper-and-pen exercise or a practical lesson. When you design your assessment program, be sure to include a few formative assessments for a quick, informal evaluation of student learning—rubrics, for example, and/or running records (used in some reading programs). Then build in the summative evaluations you plan to administer at the end of a unit, semester, or academic year. The ISTE guidelines in box 3.4 can help you plan your assessments.

BOX 3.4   ISTE standards that can help you plan your assessments as you become a TechnoTeacher

- Creativity and innovation ("Students demonstrate creative thinking, construct knowledge, and develop innovative products and processes using technology.")
- Communication and collaboration ("Students use digital media and environments to communicate and work collaboratively, including at a distance, to support individual learning and contribute to the learning of others.")
- Research and information fluency ("Students apply digital tools to gather, evaluate, and use information.")
- Critical thinking, problem solving, and decision making ("Students use critical thinking skills to plan and conduct research, manage projects, solve problems, and make informed decisions using appropriate digital tools and resources.")
- Digital citizenship ("Students understand human, cultural, and societal issues related to technology and practice legal and ethical behavior.")
- Technology operations and concepts ("Students demonstrate a sound understanding of technology concepts, systems, and operations.")

Now is also a good time to think about using the capabilities of digital media to create multimedia portraits of your students as learners, as our three TechnoTeachers did. Here are a few tools that can make the process more dynamic than paper-and-pencil evaluations. Try adapting one or more for your students.

- Use a spreadsheet to help you create an evaluation rubric. Or search the Web for digital rubric builders and modify them as needed.
- If you have already created several rubrics with your class, try using the ForAllRubrics app (free for teachers). This app will allow you to import your rubrics. You can also use it to create new ones, grade student work, and print out data.[12]
- Check out free, customizable survey tools, such as SurveyMonkey or Zoomerang, that can help you get quick feedback on how well students understand a concept.
- Use the Socrative website to generate a quick quiz by inputting your own content.
- Think of your classroom blog as a repository of student work.
- Create a wiki and have it do double-duty. A wiki can help your students connect and communicate. It can also become an archive of student work that you (and they) can evaluate. As high school science teacher Louise Maine explains, "The wiki is the hub of our lives in the classroom. It allows for changing structures in the classroom, and you can create individual or group pages." (At the end of the school year, you can archive your wiki so students can revisit it.)[13]
- Create e-portfolios of students' projects. If possible, have them take responsibility for spotlighting their best work (critical thinking at work). Far from seeing it as a chore, many students enjoy using scanners, digital cameras, DVDs, and other devices for this purpose. E-portfolios can also give students insights into the creative process. By refining and enlarging upon their ideas over time, they are following the lead of many artists, musicians, playwrights, and other creative people.[14]

Once you have completed and evaluated your first Stellar Unit, it is time to consider how you can weave this learning into the next school term, and the one after that. Hold on to your hats. It is time to move to the next stage in chapter 4. We are now planning our blueprint for the entire year.

You are now becoming a TechnoTeacher.

EXHIBIT 3.1   **TechnoTeaching Student/Group Conference Tracker**

Project _____   Date _____

Student or group members _____

Where are you now with your project?

What's working well for you or your group?

Where do you feel stuck?

What do you need to get unstuck?
- Skills & Tools (media, tools, research help)

- Content (books, online articles, interviews)

- Mindset (exploration, stick-to-it-iveness, cooperation, communication)

Next steps (e.g., share/display your work in progress; revise draft; learn how to _____):
1.

2.

3.

Next teacher check-in date (later today? two days? one week?):

Additional comments and observations:

_____

CHAPTER 4

Hunkering Down

Plan the Year Ahead

You have now planned and at least started your first Stellar Unit. You may have even completed it. In any respect, you are ready for the next Techno-Teaching adventure. In this chapter, we will show you how to develop your own blueprint for the upcoming academic year, with a year's worth of Techno-Teaching projects that you will roll out as the year progresses.

We will also show you how our TechnoWhy?, TechnoOK, and TechnoYes! teachers designed their next three Stellar Units to anchor their instruction. We will point out how, as reflective practitioners, they keep a personal log of their long-range plans and ongoing observations. (We strongly encourage you to keep a log as well.)

Above all, we will encourage you, in a step-by-step fashion, to have fun as you learn along with your students.

THE 180-DAY OR 36-WEEK CHALLENGE

In many school systems, the academic year consists of approximately 180 days. Let's suppose, just for a ballpark figure, that you plan to dedicate six weeks to one Stellar Unit. Let's also suppose that your school year design is something on the order of thirty-six weeks. Okay, then. That means you could potentially teach a maximum of six Stellar Units during the school year.

On the other hand, if you think your Stellar Unit will take eight weeks, you could teach four Stellar Units during the school year, or three long and three short. (See table 4.1 for possible combinations.)

Break out your academic calendar or journal and begin planning, using the template in figure 4.1 (which we'll cover in depth later in this chapter).

Or go digital. You can use the free Google Calendar website, which allows you to create calendars that you can adapt for your school year.[1] The home page walks you thorough the process of linking your calendar with others on your team (including mobile access if you like). Jules favors the big, wall-size calendars or whiteboards with boxes big enough to write in, while Nic likes to create colorful posters and tables on her laptop.

Invite your fellow teachers (the team of teachers with whom you worked on your Stellar Unit outline, perhaps) to join you for a planning session. If you are lucky enough to have a technology coordinator or instructional technology (IT) specialists on staff, invite them to join you, along with other movers and shakers. And remember, nothing sustains the creative process like food! Bake brownies. Brew a pot of coffee (teachers will follow the scent of coffee anywhere, right?). Or organize a combination meeting/pizza party. (Nic suggests a more British format—tea and cake.)

TABLE 4.1   **The 180-day or 36-week challenge**

Six Stellar Units	Six weeks each = thirty-six weeks
Four Stellar Units	Eight-plus weeks each = thirty-two-plus weeks
Three long Stellar Units and three short Stellar Units	Eight weeks for each long unit = twenty-four weeks Three weeks for each short unit = nine weeks Total = thirty-three weeks

FIGURE 4.1   **Week-by-week blueprint for Stellar Units**

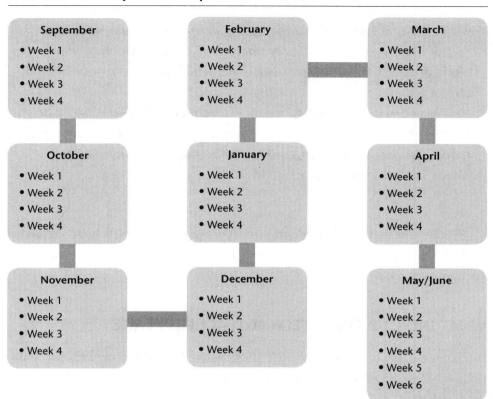

Nic advises   Take small, definite steps. Get comfortable and get confident. Focus on teaching a few curricular units really well. Having a holistic view of the school terms ahead, combined with detailed planning, will help you find a sense of calm within the chaos that is the academic year. You don't want things to creep up on you.

Plan your time knowing what hurdles you have ahead. Look at report presentation weeks, parent evenings, vacations, and exam *periods. The last thing you want to do is spend your precious weekends and holidays struggling to pull things out of a hat. This sort of frenetic activity will only add an air of desperation to your work. Students can smell fear like dogs, which will doom your best efforts before you have even begun.*

Give yourself breathing space for reinvention, reflection, and Plan Bs. Plot the details in advance and ensure you have support resources (people, rooms to teach in, and lesson activities) organized. Your future self will thank you for it.

By the end of this chapter, you and your colleagues will have created a blueprint for the entire academic year. But first let's check in on our three TechnoTeachers.

WHAT DID OUR THREE TECHNOTEACHERS PLAN?

In chapter 3, each of our TechnoTeachers kicked off the year with an ambitious multimedia project designed to set the tone for future studies. Next, they designed three more units to extend the first Stellar Unit and provide many opportunities for students to hone their skills.

Jules advises In the Stellar Units that follow, you will notice an emphasis on having students read, interpret, and write about books at all grade levels (i.e., Melissa in high school, Zayid in middle school, and Jasmine in grade four). This is intentional on our part. We want to respond to teachers' fears that a love of books and literature is getting short shrift in the information age. Students, teachers often lament, are reading only bits and pieces—tweets, *blogs, and text messages—more akin to dipping into a magazine, rather than literature and high-quality nonfiction. They are "pick and mix" readers, as the media critics say.*

We would like to show you how our TechnoTeachers strive to reverse this trend by assigning interesting and challenging texts to add breadth and depth to each unit.

TechnoWhy? Melissa's Next Three Stellar Units

One of the challenges Melissa noted in her self-assessment was to help students comprehend what they read in greater depth. She has read research articles that illustrate how short writing assignments can give students opportunities to think on paper (or digitally), and how this type of thinking can boost their ability to understand and interpret what they read.[2] With this in mind, Melissa decides her second Stellar Unit will be on student journal writing.

Second Stellar Unit: Journal writing

In the fall, Melissa teaches her high school students how to create "a double-entry journal" for the upcoming unit she's planning on historical fiction. For this type of journal, she explains, students will draw a line down the middle of the page. In the lefthand column they will write a quotation or historical fact from the novel they are reading. Then, in the righthand column, they will *interpret* what they have written.

In reading a historical novel, for example, that portrays Roger Williams, the founder of Rhode Island, as someone who tried to create positive relations with the Narragansett Indian tribe, students might copy a quotation from him on the left side of the page and then offer an opinion or interpretation of what he said on the right. They might do something similar in reading about how Rhode Island was the first British colony in America to declare its independence—two months before the Declaration of Independence was signed. How do they interpret that event? Or students might want to respond to a book about

Anne Hutchinson, a Puritan advocate of religious freedom, and her influence on Roger Williams in setting up the Rhode Island colony. What do students make of their efforts?

Melissa's students take to the journals and make them their own, using old-fashioned lined notebooks, iPad writing apps, or digital files they post to the cloud (through Google Docs, for example).

At several points during the unit, Melissa collects the journals. She writes comments and suggestions for how students can connect with broader historical themes. Sometimes she meets with individuals for mini-conferences (which include either her AEN students or her advanced students, depending on her focus) and shows them how to dig deeper in their interpretations and make connections to advanced history texts.

For students who would like to work on their journals online, Melissa learns how to set up digital journal templates, with initial questions keyed to the works of historical fiction she plans to assign. Building on her first foray into podcasts (in her first Stellar Unit), she and her students learn how to create different podcasts for different topic areas (in her case, one for each book). They use GarageBand software, which is already installed on the Macintosh computers Melissa borrowed from the IT department.

Fortunately, Melissa is now on good terms with her tech coordinator and is only slightly embarrassed to ask for help. They have conversations about the flexible nature of the double-entry journals (digital and print), which Melissa can easily imagine adapting for other units in the future.

Third Stellar Unit: Advertising historical novels

After winter break, Melissa begins a Stellar Unit on historical fiction that capitalizes on the power of peer book reviews. She has read several research articles, which indicate over and over that when students write for their peers (or a broader audience in general) their writing is much stronger than when they write solely for their teacher. Students are also more willing to edit and polish their work when they have an authentic audience. (These findings have held up across several decades—from the 1970s to the present.)[3]

The peer book review unit involves having students hone their podcasting skills to advertise the novels they enjoyed reading and convince classmates to read them too.

To get started, Melissa asks the students who created podcasts for the Newport history Stellar Unit to take the lead and create the first podcast advertising a book. Although it is a big step for Melissa to give up the reins, she definitely sees the advantages.

Fourth Stellar Unit: Publishing an interactive page on the school website

In the early spring, Melissa will investigate how to create an interactive page for the school website. As part of this project, she and her students will study a map of the area, and add links to the places/podcasts/information the students created in the fall. Then they will present their project to members of the Newport Historical Society using digital presentation tools. They will also write a description of the project and work with the Society on linking it to their web page.

Figure 4.2 offers a quick summary of how each of Melissa's Stellar Units flows into the next.

Melissa's blueprint made it fairly easy to segue from one unit to the next over a period of approximately four and a half months, not counting vacations. Even better, her colleagues have noticed that she no longer takes the Luddite point of view, and now walks with a bit of swagger (we hope).

TechnoOK Zayid's Next Three Stellar Units

Given that Zayid's middle school students studied *narrative* storytelling in their first Stellar Unit, Zayid will focus on non-narrative text structures for the next several months as per his school's benchmarks. He will also bear in mind his self-assessment plan and his goal of being more systematic (and less spontaneous) in his integration of edtech.

Second Stellar Unit: Using Internet research tools responsibly

With an eye toward high-utility twenty-first-century skills, Zayid launches a unit on Internet research tools, ethics (e.g., plagiarism, digital citizenship), and

FIGURE 4.2   **TechnoWhy? Melissa's next three Stellar Units**

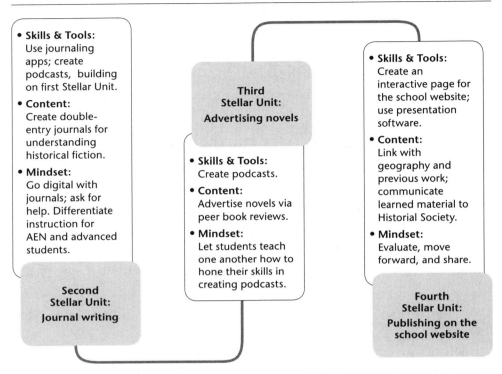

the ins and outs of fair use (public domain) photographs. Students continue to learn these skills (as they did in their first Stellar Unit) through an inquiry project called "Nonfiction: The News and Popular Press," which is one of their English and Literacy lessons. The unit culminates with each group teaching their classmates what they have learned about the news and how it is presented to the public.

Third Stellar Unit: Creating conceptual maps as a prewriting activity

In a similar vein, Zayid's next Stellar Unit focuses on conceptual mapping as a prewriting strategy. Rather than starting from scratch, Zayid takes advantage of various digital organizers that are readily available.[4] He finds that students are more willing to delve into a "messy creative process" when using digital tools. They find it easy to erase work and try again, instead of ripping up paper, rearranging index cards, and starting all over—as he used to try to get them to do (with difficulty) before he had suitable digital tools to offer them.

Zayid's research on existing tools has turned up several websites that offer ready-made organizers that students can modify for their purposes, such as ReadWriteThink. He also introduces students to Inspiration software, which allows them to create visual representations of their thinking using various design tools.[5] One of his sons shows him a free app called Inspiration Lite, which he encourages some students to use for mind mapping on iPads (see the iTunes App Store).

The substance of Zayid's Stellar Unit is for students to learn how to write a persuasive essay. Although this is a tough text genre to master, students are required to learn it according to curriculum guidelines. Zayid hopes that by having students map out their ideas in advance, their writing will go more smoothly—with more solid arguments to support a particular point of view.

Zayid also hopes that this prewriting activity will be beneficial for his EAL students. He spends time meeting with them individually, going over their conceptual maps and providing direct instruction as needed.

Fourth Stellar Unit: Publishing zines

For this unit, Zayid will have students create *zines* (self-published, low-circulation magazines) about something that is in the news this week. Zayid believes that creating the zines will improve students' writing skills and understanding of the topic, as well as give them a chance to build their multimedia skills.

Nic advises   If you are creating a school magazine, go online and see what other schools are doing. Check out free zines and find out how you can create a paperless version of one. Look at styles in current magazines and consider how you can incorporate compelling *graphics into the school magazine. If you need help in an area (e.g., layout), see who can teach you. Many software and computer stores, such as Apple, offer in-store workshops or online tutorials.*

Do not make the barriers bigger than they are. With some desktop publishing sites, you only need to click and drag. Set aside an afternoon and get on with it. Afterward, you will feel like the cat who got the cream.

For an extra challenge, Zayid encourages students to add their own soundscapes (sound effects, narration, and music) to their stories or incorporate digital slide shows or video clips.

Nic advises   Based on my experience creating a magazine in my first teaching job and managing websites over several years, I offer the following tips:

- *Consider the audience. Is the magazine for the students or their parents?*
- *Encourage the students to take ownership. Do you really need to lead everything? Can you assign a student editor (or two) from higher up in the school to oversee the editorial process for you? Delegating some of the work will not only give advanced students leadership skills, but will also give them something they can add to their future résumés or CVs that will set them apart from others.*
- *Take a trip to the local newspaper office so students can see what goes on there. Perhaps you can also arrange some work experience for students who particularly enjoy this type of project.*

All of these activities will enhance the students' learning experience, and you will pick up a few publishing tricks along the way!

Figure 4.3 illustrates how Zayid's three Stellar Units progress over the course of the school year.

By spring, Zayid's students have completed several multimedia publications (which can become part of their e-portfolios); he feels they are firing on all cylinders.

FIGURE 4.3   **TechnoOK Zayid's next three Stellar Units**

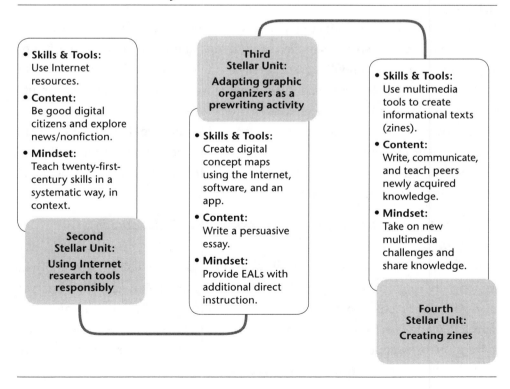

- **Skills & Tools:** Use Internet resources.
- **Content:** Be good digital citizens and explore news/nonfiction.
- **Mindset:** Teach twenty-first-century skills in a systematic way, in context.

Second Stellar Unit: Using Internet research tools responsibly

Third Stellar Unit: Adapting graphic organizers as a prewriting activity

- **Skills & Tools:** Create digital concept maps using the Internet, software, and an app.
- **Content:** Write a persuasive essay.
- **Mindset:** Provide EALs with additional direct instruction.

- **Skills & Tools:** Use multimedia tools to create informational texts (zines).
- **Content:** Write, communicate, and teach peers newly acquired knowledge.
- **Mindset:** Take on new multimedia challenges and share knowledge.

Fourth Stellar Unit: Creating zines

TechnoYes! Jasmine's Next Three Stellar Units

Building on the momentum of her keypal exchange, Jasmine designs the next three Stellar Units to take advantage of her students' interest in "meeting" other students around the world; she will also continue to use these units to deepen children's reading, writing, and thinking skills. Similar to Melissa's high school students in their third Stellar Unit, Jasmine's fourth graders will pitch their favorite books to peers near and far.

Second Stellar Unit: Pitching "Books We Couldn't Put Down"

In late October, Jasmine introduces a unit called "Books We Couldn't Put Down." The idea is that students will learn to speak persuasively about their favorite books and explain why their classmates should run right out and begin reading them. Children will also create advertising posters for their book using digital art tools.

Ultimately, Jasmine plans to post the write-ups and posters on a classroom wiki or the school website. She has a rough idea about how to go about it, but will check with the school's IT specialist to make sure that she is consistent with her school's policies on posting student work. Then she will invite parents to access the wiki to see their children's projects.

In working with her AEN students, Jasmine will ensure that all students are aware of their targets, and make certain that any school intervention feeds into this. She will use praise at all times and consider how to involve the students' families more in their learning than she has in the past.

Third Stellar Unit: Exchanging book reviews with Texas students via Skype

After winter break, students will rehearse their "book pitch" for one another. When they've got it down, they will take part in an exchange with a partner classroom in Dallas, Texas, via Skype. The children in Dallas have also prepared book pitches to send to Jasmine's class. (Jasmine and her partner teacher have already swapped lists of students' favorite books, so they can make sure to have several copies available after the Skype sessions.)

This is Jasmine's first time using Skype in the classroom. With Texas being only an hour ahead of Québec City, she and her teaching partner can easily arrange a few teleconferences.

Fourth Stellar Unit: Exchanging biographies with New Zealand students via wiki and blog

Taking the "Books We Couldn't Put Down" theme one step further, Jasmine teaches her students how to convince others to read biographies of people they admire. They begin by writing summaries of their famous person's life. After a few editing sessions, they create podcasts of their work.

For the winter book fair, some children want to dress up as their famous person and take turns interviewing each other in character. Jasmine photographs the event for the classroom wiki. Now they are ready to swap ideas (and interviews), with children from a town near Wellington, New Zealand.

The idea for this exchange was the result of a conversation Jasmine had in the fall with a like-minded teacher, David, from New Zealand. They thought it would be cool (as well as full of potential for social studies, geography, and global studies units) to have students share the life stories of the people they have been reading about and develop interview skills. Jasmine got in touch with him to make arrangements.

Figure 4.4 shows a breakdown of Jasmine's second through fourth Stellar Units.

Jasmine's fourth Stellar Unit went so well that David tries to convince her to collaborate on a presentation that they can deliver at next year's International Society of Technology Educators conference. She is trying to work up the nerve to say yes.

YOUR TURN

Which Stellar Units will you design? What would be the logical next step to follow your first Stellar Unit? How can you build student learning? Remember, the goal is to lay a solid foundation, brick by brick.

FIGURE 4.4   **TechnoYes! Jasmine's next three Stellar Units**

- **Skills & Tools:**
  Create classroom blog and wiki; use digital art tools.
- **Content:**
  Pitch "Books We Couldn't Put Down": literature and recommending books.
- **Mindset:**
  Comply with school policies on posting student work.

Second Stellar Unit:
Pitching "Books We Couldn't Put Down"

Third Stellar Unit:
Exchanging book reviews with classroom in Texas

- **Skills & Tools:**
  Use Skype.
- **Content:**
  Same as second Stellar Unit, but share book recommendations beyond the classroom.
- **Mindset:**
  Promote global learning and collaboration. Pay additional attention to AEN students.

- **Skills & Tools:**
  Use wiki and individual blogs.
- **Content:**
  Read biographies, write, learn how to interview others, and share.
- **Mindset:**
  Contribute to global learning; copresent with a colleague at an edtech conference.

Fourth Stellar Unit:
Exchanging biographies with classroom in New Zealand

Sketch out your ideas using the template in table 4.2 (and in figure 4.1) to guide you. Also, table 3.2 in the preceding chapter offers several options for you to consider, drawing from the three elements we have discussed: Skills & Tools, Content, and Mindset. (We have also added a column for your ideas for developing global consciousness in your students, a topic we take up in chapter 6.) Or feel free to devise your own system. The main goal is to narrow down your list of ideas so you can fully develop each one. It is better to do a few things well than to take on too much all at once. Then begin. No excuses—just get your head down and get started.

TABLE 4.2   **Long-range blueprint for the academic year**

When	Skills & Tools	Content	Mindset	Global consciousness
1. Mid-September through end of October				
2. November through end of December (six weeks, working around winter break)				
3. January (four weeks)				
4. Mid-February through end of March (six weeks)				
5. April through early May (six weeks)				
6. Mid-May through early June (four weeks)				

Jules advises The decisions our three TechnoTeachers made in designing their blueprints for the year represent just a small fraction of the possibilities available to you. It all depends on your particular educational context.

Creating your blueprint is more of an art than an exact science. Decide which Stellar Units will yield the biggest educational gains for you and your students. Which ones will give your students the fundamental skills that will serve them well throughout their academic careers?

If you are not sure where to begin, check with the curriculum coordinator(s) in your school. Talk about the learning goals for students at your grade level and how Stellar Units can incorporate the most important ones. Also discuss how you can lay a foundation for literacy development that will serve your students well this year and beyond (reading, writing, and communicating ideas).

Your curriculum coordinator can also guide your decisions about pacing—for example, how long should you spend on a particular unit and when is it time to move on?

If you are reading this section as a school leader, be proactive about checking in with novice teachers or others who would benefit from your background in TechnoTeaching or curriculum design. Have them look back at their self-assessments. Talk through particular standards (e.g., ISTE or CCSS) that they can draw upon. Show them how to package their ideas into projects that allow teachers and students to draw on content area knowledge as they go.

The time you spend involved in advance planning will reap huge rewards both for teacher and student learning. Share what you know so no teacher (or team of teachers) has to chart a course alone.

Choose Stellar Units Aligned with Your Goals

Following are several teaching units for you to consider adapting, each of which has a solid research base to support its benefits for students. Each unit will help lay the foundation we mentioned, and is an essential building block that will lead to academic success. In other words, if you combine these types of units with your particular goals, you can't go wrong.

- Writing projects (sustained over time)
- Journal writing in response to literature or informational articles
- Peer teaching
- Inquiry learning, using students' curiosity as a guide
- Internet research (and digital citizenship)
- Mind mapping using graphic organizers
- Communication within the school community and globally
- Development of a life-long love of literature and nonfiction
- Creative expression through the humanities (e.g., art, drama, digital graphics, photography, soundtracks, and soundscapes)

We have all seen scattershot lessons that have some educational value but no real staying power and no chance to expand, enrich, and extend student learning. The teachers we work with want more than clever apps, unfocused Internet research, and word processing sessions that are not integrated into the writing process but are mainly about "neatening up" students' messy first drafts.

To those teachers, we suggest projects such as the ones just listed, which transcend grade levels, curricular guidelines, and nationalities. They are part of the DNA of effective practice.

Review Your Blueprint

The next step is to review your blueprint with your team. Here are some questions to use as jumping-off points to frame your discussion.

- Does your blueprint sound manageable? Exciting?

- Does it offer just the right level of challenge, according to whether you have identified yourself as a TechnoWhy? TechnoOK, or TechnoYes! teacher?
- What type of backing will you need from school staff (e.g., your principal, IT person, edtech coordinator) to implement your blueprint?
- Have you factored in an assessment plan?
- What will your culminating project be?
- How will you share student work with parents and beyond school walls?

Plan It Out, Week by Week

The next step is to take your long-range blueprint and break it down week-by-week to help you develop your ideas more precisely. Use the template in figure 4-1 or use the digital calendar on your phone or computer (iCalendar, for example, or Google Calendar). Alternatively, this might be the perfect time to try out free online lesson planning tools, such as PlanBoard.[6] Some planning tools can save you hours of time by allowing you to save your lessons as PDF files, add memos, incorporate state standards for each lesson, and automatically shift your lessons if any of your classes are cancelled.

Whichever method you use, figure out the rhythm and flow of each Stellar Unit from month to month, using your blueprint to guide you. If you need more inspiration, refer back to the discussion of research-based practices in chapter 3.

REFLECT ON YOUR PRACTICE

You are a busy professional. You barely have time to plan, teach, and evaluate your lessons without spending time writing in a notebook. We've been there, too. And yet, a quick summary of what you taught, what students learned, and how it went can be an invaluable resource.

You will notice that all of our TechnoTeachers begin by researching what they are going to do and end by reflecting on their lessons after they are completed. This is part of the TechnoTeacher mindset. If you are going to work at improving your practice, be smart. Think about what you are doing, then pause and evaluate. What might we say to you about how your unit could be improved? Really see your teaching as a craft—something to be refined and revisited. And if you are going to be at school until 5:00 p.m., you might as well be doing something that engages your mind and heart. (More on analyzing your practice in chapter 8.)

If we were to distill our message from this chapter into the ideas (and the reflective mindset) we want you to take away, they would be:

- Creating a blueprint makes you a confident teacher.
- Creating a blueprint gives you power.
- When teachers work together to create and carry out their visions, their ability to impact student learning increases tenfold.

TAKE NOTES

One of the best strategies for taking your practice to the next level is to keep a record or journal of your TechnoTeaching journey. You might, for example, say to yourself, "I will spend thirty minutes of my planning period every Thursday asking myself how things are going and making a short list of the steps I need to take to make things even better. Improvements might include providing speech recognition software for my student with special needs, or sending parents a tip sheet for practicing interview skills at home."

If you like to write by hand, we recommend buying a spiral notebook, labeling it "TechnoTeaching," and dedicating it to taking observational notes on your Stellar Units. If you favor apps, smartphones, and tablets, find writing software that feels right to you. Keep a backup file. And get ready to have several "Aha!" experiences as you implement new ideas that will shed light on your teaching and learning.

In chapter 5, we will show you how to design and implement smaller-scale initiatives to complement a year's worth of Stellar Units. The combination of long-term and short-term projects will deepen and enhance your practice.

CHAPTER 5

Stretching

Dare Devil Missions and Other Short-Term Projects

Now is the time to take TechnoTeaching to the next level. In this chapter you will learn to become a TechnoTeacher in word and deed—and bring in a more adventurous spirit (back) to your teaching. Time and money are not seen as barriers here; while we agree that they might present challenges, they should not interfere with your passion for teaching. We hope that this chapter will give you some practical examples for kicking things off.

You have created your solid blueprint and you have started (or are planning to start) TechnoTeaching with your students. You have thought about the year ahead and are ready for your next challenge (or should we say *Mission?*).

This chapter is about considering the small, adventurous projects you can either incorporate into a single class period or teach in fifteen-minute intervals over a week or two. We call these *Dare Devil Missions*. In time, you may have a whole toolkit of ideas to draw upon, but as always, we like to start slowly. These ideas are focused on working in *your* school. (We will look at how you can stretch yourself beyond the school walls in the next chapter—step by step, remember.)

Some examples of Dare Devil Missions are using Flash software, giving online feedback, and videoconferencing with an expert as part of your lesson.

These are just a few of the types of missions we will encourage you to try in your classroom or school.

We all know that engaged students learn best. Passionate teachers also create effective learning environments. We have seen this in schools, time and time again. Keep it fresh, be involved, and dare to take a few risks in order to secure learning objectives. Nic has learned that providing teachers with examples of outstanding practice, along with resources or teaching strategies, can raise their game. Jules has learned that innovative teachers often face obstacles, but are resourceful beyond measure in finding ways to overcome them.

We will now explore a range of cross-curricular and thematic projects, which Nic piloted in several schools across the south of the U.K. Over the course of a school year, she was able to help teachers move from "Good" to "Outstanding" through the use of Dare Devil Missions. She witnessed firsthand how teachers' confidence increased along with their skills.[1]

Nic and her colleagues decided to launch the missions with a pioneering group of lead teachers from different curriculum areas in the secondary school (for eleven- through nineteen-year-olds) and pondered the best approach. The Dare Devil Missions were designed as short exercises for one class period— exercises that would stretch individual teachers.

In addition to the nine Dare Devil Missions that Nic has developed over the years, she and Jules also present TechnoTeaching projects such as "Theater and the Arts" and "Poetry Slam Dunk," which we will describe in this chapter. Somewhat less cutting-edge but still challenging, these edtech projects take their cues from the seasons and the academic cycle. They should be easy to work into your schedule.

You can use these missions to punctuate your Stellar Units. We will make sure all of the missions are possible for you.

DARE DEVIL MISSIONS: SMALL-SCALE EDTECH PROJECTS

Try using Dare Devil Missions with peer, small-group, and large-group learning formats, depending on your school's budget and what resources you have.

The good news is that most of the resources we suggest are free. (For more guidance, see the resources listed in appendix B.)

The Missions can be aligned with your continuing professional development. Try one or more Missions with a class and then give feedback to your peers or principal (or line manager in the U.K.). Your "lessons learned" will pave the way for others.

If you are reading this chapter as a teacher leader, encourage teachers in your district to try a few missions. Plan to visit their classrooms when they launch them, and provide an extra pair of hands. Offer to support teachers in any way you can.

Dare Devil Mission 1: Research and Try Out "Yahoo for Teachers"

The idea of this mission is to keep your eyes open for resources that are readily available. See what other teachers are doing across the globe, through "Yahoo for Teachers," for example (an offshoot of the Yahoo site that offers an online community with examples of classroom presentations, forums in which teachers learn and/or let off steam, and links to guides and templates for online work), and follow their lead initially. You may find that one of their stories makes a light bulb go off in your head. Give yourself fifteen minutes to be inspired and then write down three things you might do in your classroom based on what you find. Then choose the most exciting idea and run with it.

Dare Devil Mission 2: Use Flash Software—Any Way You Like!

Adobe Flash is a major piece of software that lets you create professional animation, yet it's one that teachers do not always incorporate fully into their teaching, websites, or skill set. Look at some online tutorials and examples of how people use Flash in the corporate world. Then consider how using it could improve your skills and those of your students.[2]

You might ask students just to play with Flash and create a short animation for a website based on your topic. Ask for volunteers to create a character for the school virtual learning environment. Or create an app for your Stellar Unit.

Investigate several of the great YouTube tutorials for the nitty-gritty of how to do things in Flash.[3] Alternatively, you can look at the Adobe Educational Leaders program, which focuses on a select group of schools worldwide; you will find several great case studies there.[4] Or investigate the Adobe Education Exchange.[5] Just search it out!

Dare Devil Mission 3: Get Inspired by an Article on the Mashable Website

Mashable.com is an inspirational, contemporary site where you can find exciting articles on current and future technology. (It is one of Nic's favorites, helping her get up-to-date with current ideas and approaches in a jiffy.)

Take fifteen minutes and see what inspires you. Then try out an idea, or present an article or discussion thread with your class. It could be a "top 10" list, with you challenging your students to identify their "top 10 educational apps." Or you can send out your favorite sites to "All Staff" in an e-mail.

You can take this mission one step further by checking out each of the top 10 apps online and trying to integrate them into your lessons over the course of the school year.

Dare Devil Mission 4: Give Online Feedback

Help students who are using a blog, or the social media site for educators, Edmodo.com, to develop their class feedback as part of a lesson. You can start by creating a specific blog for a lesson unit—a "one off," if you like—to document a topic or conduct research.

In any case, set up the blog and create an opportunity for students to comment on the topic or even rate the lesson (using comments and a five-star rating system). For example, you could set up a blog named "MrsPonsfords-Blog." You could add videos and presentations of web links that are relevant to the content you are teaching. Then, you could create a blog post asking students to add comments about your lesson. Or, if you prefer, you can incorporate a free online voting tool like MicroPoll or the popular PollDaddy.[6]

For the TechnoYes! teachers out there whose students already have individual blogs, you could post links to other students' blogs on your home page. Then ask your class to leave online feedback with Assessment for Learning, an established U.K. system of assessment used across the Key Stages (part of the National Curriculum). Students can, for example, give positive and negative feedback by incorporating two *stars* for things that have worked well in the lesson and a *wish* that illustrates what could be improved.

Supervise the initial rating session and give students a checklist for what to include. We suggest having them identify two positives and a target goal. Within these parameters, children might make comments such as those listed in box 5.1.

Research other school blogs to see what strategies have worked well for your colleagues.

BOX 5.1   "Two Stars and a Wish" feedback

Two Positives

One star = I liked the way that everyone was involved in the lesson and had a say. Sometimes it feels like the loudest people get to speak the most, but I liked hearing from everyone in the room.

Two stars = I learned more by working with someone who knew more than me. I liked that you planned this into the lesson, as I felt much more confident. I hope I can work with Nicky again.

One Target Goal

I wish that you had chosen a room to work in with better blinds. I found it hard to see the screen at times—even when you let me move seats.

Dare Devil Mission 5: Use Video Conferencing in a Lesson

Invite a guest speaker into your lesson via a webcam. Your visitor could be a professor at the local university, someone from another school, or a "mystery guest." It could even be a friend or member of the family who wants to get involved. Your mystery guest might enjoy assuming a different persona for this lesson (a grandfather who pretends to be a spy giving a secret mission, or a friend giving tips for filming videos). The sky is really the limit here. If you are trying this activity for the first time, you may want to practice first and ask someone you know—perhaps someone in your school—to role-play while you observe as a type of rehearsal.

Another option is to invite a health practitioner or doctor to provide evidence (or a Q&A session) for a medical topic. Or you might ask a local expert to be available online for a certain time period while you e-mail, instant-message, or Skype prevetted questions from students.

Think about who you have available to you and what you want to achieve. It might be that you cannot afford a field trip (due to limited resources), but you can Skype with your expert instead. The students will love it—and will likely learn a great deal too!

Dare Devil Mission 6: Ask Your Students

Go directly to the source. Ask students which emerging technologies *they* would like to use. Then, as you create your lesson plans, incorporate at least one into your Stellar Unit or as a standalone activity.

If students are allowed to use their cell phones in a lesson, they might ask you if they can try out a particular app.

Begin by asking students to write a proposal, a "show and tell," if you like. They can suggest a technological tool, give a presentation on how it works, tell its history, describe its target audience, and explain how they think using it would help them learn more about the unit you are studying.

You can then either judge their proposal yourself, have a student panel weigh in, or have a class vote. If you spend two lessons on this activity, you might find that you use the technology for only twenty minutes in total, but students will have learned a range of skills.

You can also be smart. If you want to teach a particular technique (e.g., using primary source material for teaching history or using writing frames for numeracy), have students incorporate this strategy into their presentation.

But be careful. This activity will not work if you just ask students to bring in tech devices from home (e.g., smartphones, iPads, e-books). They will want to spend a lesson just playing and chatting about it.

Keep your lesson structured and focused on learning outcomes. Make sure that you are the one who determines how the lesson will proceed.

Nic advises Be aware that students will bring their tech devices to school. All schools are different, but if you want to make sure everything runs smoothly, remember to ask parents for permission and to relinquish any responsibility on your part.

Also make sure that students hand you their tech devices (or bring them to the school's reception area, where they can be locked away) at the start of the day. Remind them that their cool tools are to be used for a lesson, not playtime.

Dare Devil Mission 7: Explore Online Videos and Other Web-Based Resources

When it comes to continuing professional development (CPD), many websites offer videos of master teachers and resources that you can download for your classroom. If you are a teacher trainer, you are probably aware of quite a few. These sites can supplement the CPD program for you and your team.

Some schools use the honor system, which allows teachers to keep a timesheet of their professional development. Activities can include:

- Spending a few hours watching tutorials online.
- Being part of a teaching forum (such as a website for educators).
- Participating on a social media site. You can, for example, search Twitter for #edchat, which tweets topics relevant to U.S.-based educators, or #UKedchat, which hosts an online chat between U.K.-based teachers on Thursday evenings.
- Taking part in a workshop halfway across the country.

There are a number of websites—such as "Better Learning with ICT: Online Communities in the Classroom"—that can help you learn about best practices in other schools.[7] These sites often include case studies of teachers who are using innovative strategies right now. You can get ideas that have been proven by others and then give it a go yourself.

The important thing to remember is that you must cater to *your* audience and ensure that you have access to similar resources, time with the students, and specific learning outcomes. Otherwise, you might find yourself using a crowbar to fit another person's ideas into your classroom, and the project will simply fall on its face. (Or you will.) A TechnoTeacher must "own it," as they say, not by just copying what others have done, but by using others' ideas to craft something for his or her situation.

Dare Devil Mission 8: Use an Interactive Whiteboard

With this mission, the idea is to motivate as many students as you can to get out of their chairs and really *use* the interactive whiteboard (which often just sits idle in the back of the room).

Begin with a fun activity where you challenge yourself to get as many students as possible out of their seats, up at the board, and finding solutions to problems for themselves.

There are several ways you can go about using the whiteboard. You can create resources yourself, invent timed activities, or ask students to create a series of games, resources, and/or activities for one "fun" lesson.

Be sure to create a code of conduct first and have ways of bringing the class together quickly.

Nic advises To help with classroom management, take your cues from subject areas that specialize in dealing with lots of activities and commotion. Observe drama and sports lessons, for example, to get ideas. In those subject areas, a raised hand can mean "be quiet and stand still"; a whistle or a clap of the hands can signal the same message.

Dare Devil Mission 9: Discover a New Educational Website for Improving Teaching and Learning

Have you had a chance to review some of the free, award-winning websites that have been gaining an international audience? Set a goal for yourself to review one or more sites that can both inspire you and save you many hours of creating your own resources. It's amazing how many outstanding educators have made their work available to the world at large. Here are a few suggestions to get you started.

- *TED Talks: Education (www.ted.com/topics/education).* With the tagline "Ideas Worth Spreading," TED Talks have won acclaim across industries. Check out a few of Sir Ken Robinson's "10 Talks on Education"; Daphne Koller on learning from online education; Shabana Basij-Rasikh on educating Afghan girls; Daphne Bavelier on "Your Brain on Video Games"; and dozens more.
- *Khan Academy (www.khanacademy.org).* Khan Academy has a mission: to provide educational videos (over four thousand three hundred) on topics including K–12 math, science, and the humanities. Each video is approximately ten minutes long, with lectures and visuals. The site also offers problem sets (with hints and supplementary videos) and tracks student learning. The cost? Zero.

- *Edudemic (www.edudemic.com)*. Edudemic keeps its finger on the pulse of innovative teaching with articles about flipping classrooms, improving your school media skills, integrating iPads into the classroom, and turning your iBook into a video—just for starters. If you find this site intriguing, you can sign up for a free daily e-mail edtech blast.
- *ReadWriteThink (www.readwritethink.org)*. Developed by the International Reading Association and the National Council of Teachers of English, ReadWriteThink offers professional development, articles about the latest edtech research, classroom resources, parent and afterschool materials, and more.

THE THREE TECHNOTEACHERS AND THEIR TECHNOLOGY MISSIONS

Read the following examples of our three TechnoTeachers' Dare Devil Missions, and consider which Mission you would choose, and which Mission someone else might choose for you.

TechnoWhy? Melissa's Dare Devil Mission

Let's check in with TechnoWhy? Melissa in Newport, Rhode Island. Having already hit her high-water mark this year with her Stellar Units, Melissa is not sure she wants to take on any additional technology challenges. Mimi, the professional development guru in the high school where Melissa teaches, convinces her that it's just a one-shot activity—no big deal—unlike her photo essay project and the other Stellar Units she taught during the year. Mimi inserts three different options inside an envelope, specifically designed for Melissa.

When Melissa opens the envelope, she finds the following three options.

7. *Watch an online channel.* Become familiar with online sites and resources for educators.
8. *Use an interactive whiteboard.* Have students solve problems by working together at the interactive whiteboard.

9. *Discover a new educational website.* Search for the best websites to help improve teaching and learning.

Melissa wants to be dynamic—but privately. She decides to look at the last Dare Devil Mission on the list, number 9, and search for a new educational website. She is thrilled when she finds a subscription-based resource site that will support her curriculum—Edusites (an online resource in the U.K. that supports educators of English, media, and film).

Melissa had heard about the free sites, but they often did not allow for differentiation and were generally "death by work sheet," as the younger teachers said. Edusites not only gives her information and tips, it also empowers her to adapt the material for her own students (some of the materials are free; some are subscription-based). The site offers schemes of work to download plus articles aimed at teachers to cover all the information on a particular topic, without their having to Google it.

Using Edusites, Melissa begins her search for one scheme of work she is considering: incorporating film into her module. She has no idea where to start. This site is full of ideas for teaching a whole film or viewing a representation or reenactment of an event. She chooses the representation since rather than having students watch an entire film. Essentially, she wants them to learn about a time in history depicted in a film.

Melissa clicks around to see what inspires her. She then adds the best of the online resources she finds to her existing topic. Next she plans to review the resources before presenting them to students, to get a head start on thinking of creative ways to improve their learning. With nudges from her daughter, Daisy, Melissa even considers allowing her class to go on the site to choose the materials they like the best.

TechnoOK Zayid's Dare Devil Mission

Back in the middle school where Zayid teaches in Bournemouth, England, a member of the leadership team gives him three envelopes, each containing a Dare Devil Mission. She asks Zayid to give it a go and give his feedback at a department meeting. The Missions are:

4. *Give online feedback.* Have students use a blog or Edmodo to develop their class feedback.

5. *Use videoconferencing.* Use videoconferencing—via Skype, for example—to invite a guest speaker to join your lesson.

6. *Ask your students.* Let students weigh in on the technologies *they* would most like to use.

Given to innovation and test-driving new tools, Zayid opts for Dare Devil Mission number 6, "Ask Your Students." He is curious about which emerging technologies they would like to experiment with and is willing to try out two or three.

He also views this Mission as way to change the behavior of a slower-paced working group, with lots of male gamers and gossipy girls. Using the technology tools will be the reward.

Zayid begins by creating a positive behavior system called "Golden Time." Students all start with thirty minutes every two weeks. Each day, Zayid takes "time" off for lateness, disruptive behavior, or anything else that detracts from the lesson.

At the end of each two-week period, Zayid lets students have Golden Time, according to how well they performed. Students who still have the full time they were allotted (thirty minutes) are allowed to do something fun. Typically, this means they get to use one of the technologies nominated, the name of which gets pulled from a hat.

Students who have used up all their Golden Time will either be given a catch-up lesson or a detention-style session, depending on how and why they used up their time.

The Golden Time strategy helps Zayid stay on track with focused learning; he loses very little time due to lateness, bickering, and student rivalries and instead can celebrate positive behavior. The Golden Time strategy also allows Zayid to circle the room, engage with students, and have one-on-one time with everyone, so not all is lost!

Some weeks, the students bring in their own devices from home. Other times, Zayid accesses the tech tools he plans to use on his school laptop. The edtech activities he has used in the past include using game consoles for a competition, listening to YouTube music videos, creating a fashion or sports blog, and using cell phone cameras.

For this particular Dare Devil Mission, Zayid challenges the group to nominate apps that can support their reading of particular texts. Specifically, he wants to see if it is easier to read Shakespeare plays online or in a book. He is also interested in whether there are any apps to help teach the dramatic aspects of speech that are hard to convey in textbooks. In addition, he wonders whether there is an app that illuminates the historical aspects of *To Kill A Mockingbird* or whether students would be better off using traditional resources. He and his students will investigate these questions and then debate the pros and cons.

TechnoYes! Jasmine's Dare Devil Mission

Meanwhile, back in Québec City, Jasmine, an avid reader of technology websites—eSchool News (www.eschoolnews.com), for example—and her school's IT specialist talk about which of these missions she might choose:

1. *Research and use Yahoo for Teachers.* Find out what resources are already out there that might be useful.
2. *Use Flash software any way you like.* Find out different ways to use Flash by watching online tutorials.
3. *Be inspired by an article on the Mashable website.* Read about the current and future of technology to get inspired.

Dare Devil Mission number 3, "Be inspired by an article on the Mashable website," captures Jasmine's interest. She initially gives herself an hour to look at the articles featured on Mashable and find out the latest tech trends, from wearable technology to cars that drive themselves (!). She has a group of her fourth graders in mind for advanced edtech work, but also wants to challenge herself.

Jasmine zeroes in on an article about web apps and music for television and film. She asks a small group of disengaged boys (some of whom are her AEN students) if they want to start a lunchtime club to learn how to use some of these apps (from the electronic loop machine GrooveMaker to the sheet music and four-part harmony of PraiseHymns) to create music for the school play.[8] They do! She lets them eat lunch with her in the classroom, and gets to know them better as they figure it out. They get a real buzz out of learning about new genres of music and mixing them together using the computer audio-editing software Audacity.[9]

Jasmine also teaches the children how to use the school lighting room, ensuring they are fully trained technicians, and eventually gets them involved in filming the play. They are now the cool kids. They call themselves "Da Crew."

HOW DID OUR THREE TECHNOTEACHERS SCHEDULE THE DARE DEVIL MISSIONS AND WHAT DID THEY LEARN?

Working and Learning from Others: Our TechnoTeachers and You

An important lesson we have learned when mentoring teachers is that flexibility and peer support are also key to a change in Mindset—a "buddy" can help you find your feet. If you have a colleague in another school whom you speak to more often than those in your building, you may wish to do a joint project.

You and your colleague could start *big* with a schoolwide, whole-curriculum "Dare Devil Mission Day" or "Small-Scale Project Workshops." Or you may just call it a "TechnoTeaching Event" (our favorite!). Decide how you want to launch the idea and then work on how staff (or you) could add what you learn to your toolkit. Decide on a timeline. What follow-up events will you organize so teachers can describe their experiences with their students?

As always, the choice is yours. Remain positive and remember to think about what you have learned from this experience.

Jules advises When you become involved in new activities, you will discover that you are good at something. It could be the dare itself, a creative approach to teaching and learning, or a *way of exciting and engaging a class. This discovery can become a catalyst for a teaching and learning dialogue. If it goes wrong, you can have a different sort of dialogue—one that encourages experimentation and support. The missions discussed next are not just "projects," but are also a means for you to engage students and improve your practice.*

THE YEAR AHEAD: INJECTING TECHNOLOGY INTO TRADITIONAL PROJECTS

We realize that the Dare Devil Missions are "daring." We know that we are asking you to take risks and to throw yourself outside of your comfort zone. We know some readers will get a real buzz out of this, and some . . . well, won't.

Therefore, we wanted you to undertake a mission that would illustrate the TechnoTeacher Mindset, but also keep your feet on the ground. The next section of this chapter is based around the idea of bringing in common elements of lesson planning—the seasons and the calendar months—and introducing a few ideas to help your lessons become "small-scale projects." We hope all of you will find a range of inspirational ideas so that you will feel you can weave at least one new TechnoTeaching element into your planning.

SMALL-SCALE PROJECTS USING THE SEASONS AND THE ACADEMIC CYCLE

Although it's a more traditional approach, you can use the months and/or seasons to inspire you. This does not have to be boring. Far from it! This inspiration could lead to launching a competition, based on the weather or key dates in the calendar, to inspire students' creativity. Or you could find competitions or events that are already up and running, and encourage your students to submit their projects.

If you are an English or history teacher, for example, you can focus on Shakespeare's work in April (his birth and death dates are both estimated as the twenty-third). You can also use history sites to research what happened on "This Day" for a moving image piece or podcast.[10]

Here we will look at some possibilities for each month, some resources, and a few suggestions that you can personalize for your classes. Review the blueprint that you created in chapter 4 and let that be your guide. Consider where you might want to be more daring. This is your plan, so be as flexible as you dare!

September: The World Around Us

Get oriented to your town, region, and continent or part of the world through Google Maps.[11] Then introduce Scribble Maps and have students annotate the maps that they find the most interesting.[12]

Younger children can work in teams making a map of the town on a multi-media blog, while older students can create their own multimedia podcast about the origins of a building.

October: Theater and the Arts

Another way to seek out what is current is to look at your local arts and technology calendar. If you have a theatre group, cinema, or recording studio near you, it would be a great idea to approach them and see what they can offer you.

By searching through a theatre's listings, you will find a range of shows that might relate to your students (either for entertainment, for exposure to the arts, or to link with a part of their curriculum). This show can then be the starting point for a reading of the book or play, an animation, a marketing campaign, or set or prop design.

The fact that this event is local, and you are part of a school, means that you can ask for special treatment! See if the actors will meet the students, or if you can get the students close to the props. You never know until you ask!

November: Me, Myself, and I

For this activity, you will ask students to represent themselves. Their project could take the form of a family history where they interview family members, or an installation they create that reflects their personalities (both their external personality that the world sees, and their internal personality that only they know, which works especially well with teenagers).

The final product can be a digital book, film, or piece of music that captures them and explains their ideas. It could also be a portrait created with moving images or photography, perhaps on a "Day in the Life" theme. Consider how you will exhibit their work, perhaps with an end-of-term "Oscars" ceremony, or a photography exhibition at the local cinema.

December: Holidays Around the World

Bringing in a global influence, students could "share" a holiday by researching different aspects of a country or city using their computers. Or you can come up with the "Top 10 Things to Do" in another place. Students can visit websites like Rough Guides and Trip Advisor to see what locations tourists enjoy.[13]

To extend the lesson, ask students to look at trends in travel or "meet up" with someone as part of Skype Classroom.[14] You might have students focus on a research project in which they learn more about a culture different from their own (perhaps a classmate's) or their own ancestral roots, or find out what makes their hometown appealing to tourists. There are so many ideas! The latter one is a strong project, as it allows children to look at what their town offers in terms of history, entertainment, and escapism. It also means you can get people—say, a librarian or a shopkeeper—to help. Someone who has lived in the town and is keen to tell his or her story (perhaps a graduate of your school) may also be happy to help.

January: Winter Sky

Have students learn about the stars, planets, and the sky at night. Sites like Kids Astronomy and the BBC Learning Zone are good places to start.[15] Projects could include students' own night sky "diaries" (using photography or video) and Internet research on planets and constellations that are prominent in the winter sky. They might also look at the folklore behind the names of stars, planets, and constellations, and consider space travel.

February: Silent Movie

Silent movies offer a good way to start working with other teachers in other departments. One class can create a piece of music based on a theme (time period, speed, or a sound effect like rain or heavy footsteps) or an emotion (fear, happiness, love, or excitement). The other class then creates a narrative for this brief scenario, perhaps summing up the title in ten words or creating a storyboard.

Next, the class can create a moving image sequence based on the music, which can then become the soundtrack. Invite students and families to a "gala" night where students share their work.

March: Arty Party

Take a tour of art museums around the world and then have students become curators of an exhibit. Begin by visiting Google Art Project. Have students take virtual tours of major art museums all over the world and select pieces for their own collections, which they can then share with others.[16] Guide students in selecting a historical art movement (Renaissance or Surrealism) or type of artwork (sculpture or oil paintings) as a framework for their collection.

April: Poetry Slam Dunk

Link the idea of creating podcasts with a "poetry slam" in April to celebrate National Poetry Month. You can use an app like WordMaker to get started, or research the oral tradition and modern poetry online as part of the project (based on a country, time period, or culture, for example).[17] Visiting one of several free poetry sites is a great way to get started. At Poets.org, for example, you can tap into a section designed for teachers and read poems by Dylan Thomas, e.e. cummings, Langston Hughes, William Blake, and Elizabeth Bishop, to name a few.[18] As of this writing, there are tips from poets on how to teach imagery using selected poems for inspiration.

You could use either class time or an assembly to host the Poetry Slam Dunk. Get an *American Idol/X Factor*–style panel together with some teachers and students (at least *one* must be dressed up like Simon Cowell!). Or invite staff, parents, and students to a "poetry slam" evening. Ask people to wear black turtlenecks (polar necks), play jazz, and bring in organic food to share. If you are more athletically inclined, combine the "Dunk" with a basketball game. Alternatively, Skype with another school and have rounds online, then take part in the final round at a café.

May: Land, Sea, or Sky

Choose a curricular topic and ask students to research different areas—land, sea, or sky. Have them research the flora and fauna (natural geography) or cultural stories (English literature or history) of the geographic region where they live.

If they choose the sea, for example, you could have them start by looking at the fish in Australia, the aboriginal stories around Uluru, and the relationship between the land and water in and around the Outback. Students who select fish in Australia can do research by viewing documentaries, visiting online aquariums, and listening to an expert speak about various species (via a video conference).

Those who investigate land might zero in on Africa. If so, have them consider animal folklore or the relationship between man and the earth.

For the sky, you might have students study astronomy—the solar system, deep space, space flight, and the universe.[19] You could also have them investigate weather, birds, or the "heavens," either where you live or someplace they would like to visit some day. There are so many options!

June/July: Personal Project

Tell students they can research a topic of their choice (with your permission). Consider how you will support them with keywords, a time period in which to research (say, twenty minutes), and a recording method so they will be ready to present their work to the rest of the class in September.

Younger children can investigate a sport, country, fashion designer, or celebrity of their choice. Older students can investigate a university, country, genre of film, music, or a theory or concept. In either case, give students a list of skills you would like them to include (based on what they have learned over the year) and ideas for presenting their projects.

MORE FORTY-FIVE-MINUTE TEACHING "EVENTS"

Now you're ready to plan one to two forty-five-minute TechnoTeaching activities per month. Grab your notebook or laptop and keep a log of which activities were a "one time only" experience (as in never again!), and which ones you will add to your toolkit. While you are at it, ask students to write a couple of sentences about the activities they thought were the most worthwhile, interesting, and fun. You may want to have them post their ideas to a wiki or blog. That way, you will have a valuable record of a year's worth of Dare Devil Missions and related projects.

SHARING BEST PRACTICES

Speak to your principal and see how you can share your experiences with others both inside and outside of your staffroom. Decide what works best: a simple "All Staff" e-mail, or a professional development event. Either can be a means of describing what you have learned from your mission(s)—both trials and successes.

If you host a meeting, consider adding some structure, such as a note-taking sheet, graphic-organizer ranking activities, or a form for sharing one really cool learning activity. Consider how you wish to present this. You might use blank envelopes containing the missions; or perhaps a "speed dating" setup so staff can share their experiences quickly and with many; or you could make a short professional development video. The point is to speak to others, spread your enthusiasm, and illustrate that being "daring" is enough. It adds a bit of passion in the classroom and can reignite those who are losing their "spark."

Jules advises If you are reading this chapter as a school leader, think about how you can create a school environment in which teachers feel excited about sharing their ideas and experiences based on Dare Devil Missions and other short-term projects.

Set the tone by being positive and discouraging the tech-averse. Show teachers who feel pressed for time how they might be able to rearrange their schedules and blueprints so they can fit in short-term activities during the arc of the academic year. Perhaps use an actual blueprint from one of the teams you have worked with that shows how teachers' ideas evolved, and how their long-range planning paid off.

Make it clear to all school staff how much you value innovative teaching that helps children become twenty-first-century learners. Leave your door open for strategy sessions. Provide as much time and as many resources to these types of endeavors as you can possibly manage.

If we think about how each of our TechnoTeachers fared in this chapter, we have to ask how they deepened and developed their practice, bearing in mind their goals for the year. First, we have TechnoOK Melissa, who at first resisted the idea of a Dare Devil Mission. She had all she could handle, she thought, with integrating digital tools into her history curriculum for the very first time. What swayed Melissa was the idea of punctuating these longer lessons with something short, an assignment that would force her to spend time researching a new educational website from the U.K. (Edusites). Melissa loves research. And she discovered that there were legions of other teachers who shared her interest in photography, history, and film. The exercise, although hardly finished in a single class period (*is anything worthwhile ever?* she thought) opened her eyes to endless possibilities for sharing ideas and resources with other educators around the world. For Melissa, this activity hit on all three elements: Skills & Tools, Content, and Mindset. She was intrigued and has already found several resources she plans to integrate into her Stellar Units.

Consider TechnoOK Zayid's experiences with the "Ask Your Students" activity. Rather than leaving the question completely open-ended, Zayid and his students searched for websites and apps that enlivened the reading of classic texts through drama, reenactments, and glossaries for Old English terms (both in Shakespeare's plays and texts such as *Beowulf*, for example). Students dug in immediately and came up with a staggering number of resources that they felt would help them and other students like them. In fact, they were so excited about what they found that they asked if they could create a page for the school website. That way, the students who are studying *To Kill a Mockingbird* (or another text assigned for homework) can access resources that are engaging and have the potential to deepen their comprehension of what they read.

Zayid gained the most in Skills & Tools—no surprise there, since that was the focus of the mission. But he also felt that he was more aware of tools that can support his Content (i.e., literature) and Mindset (how he can better help all students access the curriculum).

TechnoYes! Jasmine was only too happy to explore the Mashable website. She is always interested in working at the cutting edge; this is as good a place as any to find it. And it made one of her guilty pleasures, surfing the Web, legitimate! During the class period, she did in fact get inspired. She sped through "Top 10 Tech" for the week, "15 Easy Steps for Evaluating Your Life," and "How to Create Your Favorite Instagram Filters in Photoshop." She mentally spent hundreds of dollars on the latest gadgets and gizmos.

Forty-five minutes into the activity, Jasmine was seized by a pang of guilt. Although she was getting excited about what she was learning, she hadn't found anything she could apply to her teaching. Was it enough to just stay current? Maybe. Then she found an article on a piece of technology a student invented that can prevent cellular network overload. She posted it under

"Today's Interesting Article" on her chalkboard. Later she will share it with students. When asked to reflect on her Dare Devil Mission, Jasmine felt she had gained the most in the area of Mindset. Growth in the other two elements would follow.

We dare *you* to get started . . . now.

In chapter 6, the opportunity to look outside of your school is waiting for you, with our support and advice. With global links and webcams, the distance between classrooms is nonexistent. You may eventually find you spend more time "in a classroom" on the other side of the world than you do at the other schools in your community.

CHAPTER 6

Branching Out

Connecting Locally and Globally

You have been stretching yourself, first with ambitious Stellar Units (perhaps as many as six in year one) as well as Dare Devil Missions and other small-scale projects. You may have just been reading about these projects so far, or have decided to act on them chapter by chapter. Either way, it is time to train the spotlight on yourself and your students. How can you begin using technology to reach out to others around the world and develop a global consciousness within your school community?

Nic started reaching out by talking to teachers in her staffroom as a novice teacher. Being fairly solution-focused by nature, she got a real buzz out of trying to help others. Her advice ranged from offering a few pointers on students with low-level disruption issues to getting other members of the teaching staff onboard with edtech. Following this, she quickly moved from working *within* to *across* schools, connecting staff between geographical regions and in the realms of cyberspace.

Having once complained of being a wallflower at the Twitter party, Jules can now (with effort) express herself in just 140 characters. As with legions of other Twitter enthusiasts, she has tweeted her way into the world of school leaders, edtech developers, children's media designers, and policy makers, all from her smartphone. She has also been invited to give webinars to early childhood educators, literacy and technology enthusiasts, and school improvement advocates. The number of educators she's been able to teach digitally exceeds the number of people she's taught in person, through graduate seminars, by at least a factor of a hundred. And while she didn't get to actually meet members of the audience, many of them communicated with her in real time using iChat (built into the webinar software), and later, via e-mail.

Exchanging ideas with educators internationally and developing global consciousness are goals that call into play a mixture of Skills & Tools (starting with questions about what software or apps can you use), Content (seeing the world in new ways; helping pupils become actors on the world stage), and Mindset (asking, *How can I be sure I'm not putting students at risk? Is it worth it?*).

Jules advises In truth, the idea of "going global" can be daunting for even the most forward-thinking TechnoTeacher. There are so many ways to connect, and so little time. Once you do open up your classroom to ways of seeing the world, you will likely need to confront issues involving prejudice, human rights, and global warming.

Proceeding from the theories of international researchers such as Howard Gardner and Marcelo M. Suárez-Orozco, we explain to you how connectivity among children and adolescents can be a positive force, helping to eradicate prejudice and cultural misunderstandings.

One more thing: setting goals for global citizenship for your students is completely in keeping with the International Society of Technology in Education (ISTE) standards, and the Common Core State Standards (CCSS) in the United States, as well as guidelines under development in the U.K. Leading forces in education today, the world over, are setting an agenda for enlarging students' experience and broadening their perspective on an international scale.

Chief among these leaders is President Barack Obama, who has remarked: "Students need to be globally competent . . . The future is here. It's global, multicultural, multilingual, and digitally connected. If we put the world into world-class education, not only will we be more successful and innovative in the global economy, but we will also lay an important foundation for peace and a shared global future."[1]

We will show you how you can take the idea of connectivity one step at a time, and quickly gain confidence. We will look to the many professionals who liaise online without ever meeting face-to-face. In fact, this is exactly how we originally "met" and ended up writing this book. At the heart of our relationship was a shared passion for teaching and learning. Our entire collaboration has taken place through video conferencing, e-mails, and web links. International networking groups allowed us to branch out beyond our home countries without racking up bills for plane tickets, hotels, and conferences. Global communication is not only greener, it's *smarter*.

If we can do it, so can you. Today you can use a search engine or find a video posted online to learn about anything you need, from folding a T-shirt to learning to blog. The Web really is our guide to the universe. Now let's turn the spotlight on you.

MAKE AN ACTION PLAN

To get started, first think about an action plan as an integral part of your blueprint for the year. You might design one that becomes more and more ambitious as the academic year unfolds. Begin by reflecting on what you want to accomplish through a virtual learning community. (See the note-taking template at the end of this chapter.) Use these questions as a catalyst:

- *Which online groups would be a good match for your interests?* Check around. Read a few of the discussion threads to pick up the vibe of each group. Target one or two groups where, over time, you might begin to feel at home. Sign up today.

- *What will be the focus of your networking?* What do you want to learn from others, and what do you plan to contribute? As with the three TechnoTeachers, you need to have a clear goal in mind. That way, you will feel productive and will be more likely to follow through.

- *How much time can you spare to participate in your online communities each week?* Can you manage fifteen minutes every Tuesday and Thursday during planning time? Or a half-hour once a week after school? Figure out what works best for you and protect that time by entering it into your calendar. Be realistic so your goal doesn't become a burden. Remember, spending even just twenty minutes a week, if you do so consistently, could lead to fascinating results like partnering with children in a "sister city" or practicing a foreign language students are learning with native speakers.

- *Do you feel ready to have your students take on a global project?* If so, is there another teacher you can team up with? Is there a way to get parents involved?

- *Are you willing to share your online life with colleagues?* Think about organizing a lunchtime workshop, for example, and invite fellow teachers who are interested in making global connections. Your hook can be a promise to share a few of your exchanges with teachers you have met virtually. What type of reciprocal learning took place? What problems and dilemmas did these educators help you address?

An overview of your international projects may motivate others to give one of them a try. The more we help our students gain a sense of the larger world, the more we can help level the playing field for everyone.[2]

Nic advises If you are still not sure how to start, look to the people you know outside of the classroom. Link up with friends and/ or family abroad and see how you can talk to them. Try to swap photos (e.g., through e-mail, Flickr, or Instagram) or set up a videoconference (e.g., via Skype). Once you've gotten your feet wet, you can venture out into large online communities (where you will be one of many voices) until you feel confident enough to chat with strangers on a one-on-one basis.

Another way to look at the idea of connecting is that it is a bit like dating or being at a large teacher conference. We are normally happy to share a few words with someone at a bar, or while waiting in line at the buffet. Why not share a few words with someone in another part of the country? Most teachers are lovely, as you know, and the ones who are interested in reaching out are likely to be as open-minded and daring as you. Give them a chance. You have everything to gain.

The experiences of Fearghal Kelly, a biology teacher and learning coach at a high school in East Lothian, Scotland, sheds light on how telecommunications can enlarge one's practice.[3] When he began his career ten years ago, the only teachers he knew were those in the school in a town he had just moved to in the south of England. "Professional isolation isn't a big problem if you work in a large and vibrant school where the staff and the leadership team are innovating and have open minds to change," he says. "However, not all schools are like this. Too often teachers have found themselves in schools where innovation can be a dirty word."[4]

As part of his evolution, Kelly began blogging, then tweeting, and then joining other educators around the world. He is now part of productive communities, where he and fellow teachers can go into much greater depth than the 140 maximum characters in tweets.

"We can't just share the end product and hope other teachers can apply it in their classrooms also," Kelly says. "We need to share why we did it, how we did it, and what went wrong along the way . . . [we need to] be prepared to be positively questioned and challenged by others in the community."[5]

Before we move ahead, let's take a step back and think about young people today—millennials, if you will—and how, and how often, they connect with digital media.

STUDENTS AS DIGITAL MEDIA ENTHUSIASTS AND GLOBAL CITIZENS

Why do TechnoTeachers need to care about making global connections for themselves and their students? One reason is that many students are already operating as global citizens, and classroom lessons must reflect that reality to be relevant to students. They need to show students how to connect globally in productive ways that are appropriate and informed by facts.

Let's begin with an awareness of the jaw-dropping amount of time children spend immersed in new media. According to Common Sense Media, in the United States "children spend more time with media and digital activities than they do with their families or in school, which profoundly impacts their social, emotional, and physical development."[6] What are the cultural implications of all these hours spent interacting with screens and other digital tools?

One implication is that students, whether they are playing chess or reading zines created by adolescents in other countries, are learning to become global citizens. International educators Marcelo M. Suárez-Orozco and Carolyn Sattin shed light on what we mean by that: "Globalization is the ongoing process of intensifying economic, social, and cultural exchanges across the planet. It is an ancient dynamic that perhaps originated sixty thousand years ago when humans first embarked on a journey that would take us, as a species, out of the African savanna to explore and transform the globe . . . Globalization is about exchanges of cultures that make the old boundaries, as well as the aspired cultural coherence and homogeneity of the nation-state, increasingly untenable."[7]

Few would disagree that this "ancient dynamic" is expanding school boundaries in unprecedented ways. Even the briefest of chats with children reflect their familiarity with the countries their classmates come from, an appreciation of various religious holy days (Passover, Ramadan, and Greek Orthodox Easter, for example), and knowledge of national customs (such as the Japanese Tea Ceremony).

Regardless of where they live, today's children dress in similar fashions around the world, share a passion for international performers (consider South Korean performer Psy and the way his videos went viral), and sports heroes (such as British soccer champion David Beckham, who had millions of fans, both home and away, throughout his career).[8]

Globalization is part of the fabric of children's daily lives today. By the time they are ready for college, some 2.2 million students will study abroad every year, with a 9 percent annual increase.[9] School systems up until now have been glacial in responding to these profound changes.

Developing Global Consciousness

How can educators respond to these fast-paced changes occurring all over the world? International researchers Veronica Boix-Mansilla and Howard Gardner, as part of Harvard's Project Zero, have developed a helpful framework. After extensive research with teachers and schools, Boix-Mansilla and Gardner coined the term *global consciousness* to describe the process that leads to a stronger sense of the world we inhabit. Specifically, global consciousness is "the capacity and inclination to place our self and the people, objects, and situations with which we come into contact within the broader matrix of our contemporary world."[10]

Global consciousness has the following three dimensions:

- *Global sensitivity*, the ability to shift from a local perspective to wider viewpoints on the planet. Classroom activities that incorporate film, music, and advertising, for example, are excellent vehicles for discovering the interconnectedness between cultures as well as the tensions they underscore (e.g., prejudice and social unrest).

- *Global understanding,* the ability to think in flexible ways about developments that impact the world. It is only by understanding how the world works that students can develop the critical thinking skills they need to make sense of the rapid changes in society.
- *Global self-representation,* the growing sense of belonging to the planet as a member of the human race, with a shared humanity. Students learn to see themselves as actors on the world stage; they come to understand that the decisions they make about the environment, and the products they buy, have global implications.[11]

Later in this chapter, we will show you how our three TechnoTeachers have adapted the global consciousness framework. We will also introduce you to a few international projects that may inspire you to achieve global consciousness in your classrooms and schools. But first, we'll offer a brief overview of where we currently stand with new technologies to paint a picture that shows how ubiquitous technology has become in today's society.

Connecting Through Technology

How many people the world over are actually connected, and how?

In the U.K. Internet users constitute 82.2 percent of the population.[12] Worldwide, according to Edudemic, Internet growth over the past twelve years (2000–2012) has soared, with over 1 billion subscribers in Asia alone. The biggest increase has been in Africa, where the number of Internet users has risen by 3,000 percent over the past ten years.

Although these statistics are encouraging, there is still a sizable gap between those who are connected and those who are not. Plus, even though 98 percent of U.S. homes have access to high-speed broadband, tens of millions of Americans are not yet computer literate. Some of the disparities are increasing across racial, socioeconomic, and geographic lines, with approximately 60 million people shut off from basic services and job opportunities in neglected parts of the country.[13]

One effort to redress these disparities involves the Federal Communications Commission, which has voted to invest in an improved E-Rate (federally subsidized) program for schools and libraries with state-of-the-art telecommunications service and equipment. This initiative includes high-speed Internet connections and a more economical plan for paying for services.[14]

Social media

Sir Tim Berners-Lee, inventor of the Internet, has remarked, "Although you can look at the Web as a technical system, perhaps a more reasonable or useful way is to look at it as a system for connecting humanity through technology."[15] To his point: as of 2012 half of all Internet users had signed up for a social media account (e.g., Facebook, Twitter). But how often do people, on average, tap into their accounts? Studies show that over 63 percent of those who have accounts get involved in social media at least once a month (as of 2012), with even more connectivity anticipated in the future.[16]

Social networks for teachers

If you are one of the 10 million members of Edmodo you know what we mean. Edmodo is a secure social networking website for posting students' work, collaborating with other teachers, and posting content for others. If you are not yet a member, you can easily set up a free account.[17]

Perhaps you are a member of Classroom 2.0, a community-supported network with 70,000 members from over 188 countries (as of this writing).[18] Classroom 2.0 currently offers resources on a variety of topics, a cross-disciplinary discussion of free apps to build vocabulary, and special interest groups for history and math.

If you enjoy learning from other educators via video lectures, then you may have joined the Educator's PLN, with links to TED Talks (discussed in chapter 5) and lectures.[19] These resources may give you a new way to think about current trends, such as flipped classrooms and blended learning.

Global communities for educators

You can also take a college course—absolutely free—from universities such as Harvard, MIT, and the University of Texas system through *massive open online courses* (MOOCs). Once merely a dream to help equalize educational opportunities throughout the world, MOOCs have grown over the past few years through organizations such as edX and Coursera.[20] Although people who take online courses are not eligible to earn a degree from the partner university, they can earn a certificate for having completed a course.

If you are an English teacher, you might be a member of English Companion, "where English teachers go to help each other."[21] Here, you can swap ideas with others who teach Shakespeare, share reading strategies, and discuss adolescent literature.

Ultimately, virtual communities can help level the playing field. As Ernest Morrell, a professor at Columbia University's Teacher College, says, "I'm excited because one of the breakthroughs we need in the profession is to be able to share practice so people doing great work are universally known within the profession."[22] Say goodbye to the isolation of working behind the classroom door, hoping to be recognized for excellent work. There is a new world order in place!

Technology and educational consultant Margaret Powers is a believer in building global communities. She advises teachers who want to get involved to start small. Setting up a Twitter account is a great way to find other educators to follow and make connections from among millions of users. Powers suggests that teachers look at whom *those* people are following and select a few of them to follow themselves.

Once teachers make connections through Twitter, they can take the next leap forward by participating in Twitter's real-time chats. Since many of her fellow teachers are early-childhood specialists, Powers suggests a chat specifically geared toward kindergarten teachers. They can also participate in monthly global classroom meetings.

Nic advises   Where to start? There are several virtual communities designed with the new teacher in mind. My advice would be to pick your top two and bookmark them. Allow yourself time to *thoroughly research the site (with a cup of tea, of course). Click on links to various resources based on ideas, concepts, and new whizzy things that you are very passionate about.   Or give yourself time (one to two hours, perhaps) to really surf the Web to see what is happening in the cyberworld. Try doing a Google search on the phrase "technology and the classroom," for example, and see where it leads you.*

Another way to get started is to ask a forward-thinking colleague, someone whose judgment you trust. That person can point you to a wealth of online mentors waiting to help you with top advice and suggestions about resources. You just have to ask.

Reaching out to more experienced colleagues for help is a practice that can serve you well throughout your career. Before you know it, your fellow teachers will look to you for advice (look at me!).

Accessing Virtual Communities of Practice

What, or where, are some of the other virtual spaces where you are likely to meet like-minded teachers? And once you have found them, what tools can you use to collaborate? Here are a few ideas.

- *Curriki.* An international site for free learning resources, Curriki includes news from the Curriki community, Twitter updates, blog posts, featured teachers, polls—and yes, an opportunity to collaborate with teachers from all over the world (699 groups, as of this writing).[23]
- *Pedagoo.* Share ideas with teachers, mainly from Scotland, at this site, where "risk is permitted, failure is seen as opportunity, and success is a shared not solitary opportunity." You can join a virtual community and/ or connect with other educators at TeachMeet events.[24]
- *The Guardian Professional Development Site: Teachers.* Discover a wealth of teaching resources, updates about the field from a European perspective, and opportunities for online professional development.[25]

- *Thinkfinity.* Tap into conversations with other twenty-first-century educators, digital resources from *National Geographic*, and global perspectives.[26]
- *ReadWriteThink.* Meet other educators who are committed to high-quality literacy instruction and ongoing professional development.[27]

GLOBAL CONSCIOUSNESS AND OUR TECHNOTEACHERS

Now that we've discussed some current forms of technology and how they're used to connect people worldwide, let's return to Boix-Mansilla and Gardner's global consciousness framework to illustrate a few classroom-based ideas. Again, we will turn to our TechnoTeachers and their experiences. This time, we'll start with TechnoOK Zayid.

TechnoOK Zayid: Global Sensitivity

Having grown up in Mumbai, TechnoOK Zayid is acutely aware of some of the cultural misunderstandings faced by those who, like him, have immigrated to Europe. When Zayid was a boy, a classmate once teased him about growing up near elephants, when in fact there are few elephants in India outside of remote areas.[28] Given that his one hundred fifty students represent the multi-cultural spectrum that ultimately makes up modern Britain, Zayid sees a terrific opportunity to combine two goals: developing greater cultural awareness and improving student writing. Because this project will become one of his Stellar Units, he blocks out six weeks to teach it on his blueprint for the year.

Zayid begins by creating a classroom climate in which it is okay to ask respectful questions of fellow students to gain insights into the language(s) and customs of their native lands. Next, Zayid launches a project through Skype in the Classroom, a free website that connects educators from all over the world.[29] He finds other educators who also want to help their students see that there is no "ordinary life"; everyone has different family customs and "rules." They decide to read and write about twenty-four hours in the life of students around their classroom, and around the world.

As a culminating activity, students compare the knowledge that they have gained of one another with what they discover about students in other countries. Zayid feels certain that these insights will deepen students' respect for other cultures and the different ways people make their way in the world.

TechnoWhy? Melissa: Global Understanding

Realizing that several of her high school students in Rhode Island had barely traveled beyond theirs, the smallest state, TechnoWhy? Melissa launches a digital project titled "How Travel Broadens the Mind." She plans it for two class sessions, so it is more of a Dare Devil Mission than a Stellar Unit.

All she will need technology-wise is several computers with an Internet connection and a few camcorders, all of which she has access to in the school's computer lab (if she puts in a request). She begins by having students create a wish list of things to do in other countries (see wild gorillas in Africa or bungee-jump in New Zealand, for example).

To help them better understand how travel shapes a person's character and understanding of the world, Melissa has students interview friends and family who have travelled somewhere out of the ordinary. Based on the interviews, students will contact tourist boards to research the city or town the interviewee visited. They will also collect "video evidence" to build a case for including a location-related activity on the classroom wish list.

TechnoYes! Jasmine: Global Self-Representation

When TechnoYes! Jasmine's fourth graders viewed a film about how Charles Ledbeater placed computers in the shantytowns of Brazil, and the effect it had on children's learning, they wondered how they might be able to help introduce the Brazilian children to the computer.[30] Through Skype in the Classroom, children contact classrooms in other countries, based on where Jasmine had travelled in her youth. Wanting to give justice to this topic, Jasmine frames it as a Stellar Unit and blocks out five weeks in her blueprint to teach it.

Jasmine organizes this project with other teachers via e-mail and then arranges one "test" Skype. When they are up and running, Jasmine and her students take part in a subsequent Skype meeting (twenty minutes each). Children in both countries have prepared questions in advance about learning with computers. Once they are face-to-face, students ask one another how much screen time they have in school and at home. They also ask questions about their teachers and how people use computers in school and at home.

Over time, students learn how their peers feel they learn best. They also speculate on how students might learn twenty and fifty years into the future. The ideas they come up with are the basis of their designs for classrooms of the future. These designs illustrate precisely what students think are important aspects of the classroom. They also give the teachers a window into what they enjoy about their lessons in the "present."

Jules advises One of my favorite quotations about global citizenship comes from Boix-Mansilla and Gardner: "Preparing students to thrive as members of world societies calls for teachers who view themselves as brokers between children and their rapidly changing environments—not mere conveyers of certified information."[31]

DEVELOPING GLOBAL CONSCIOUSNESS IN YOUR CLASSROOM

Now that you have a good understanding of global consciousness and have seen how our three TechnoTeachers incorporated its elements in their classrooms, you might be wondering how to promote the concept with your students. Following are several ideas to help you launch a global consciousness project in your classroom.

Take Part in an International Conversation

Organizations such as the ePals global community can help you connect with other teachers in more than two hundred countries to collaborate on projects that foster cultural understandings in several languages.[32] Sixth graders in Bakersfield, California, for example, connected to classrooms in Iceland in a show of support after a volcano erupted there in May 2011.[33]

If math is your area, your students can participate in a "Kites Around the World" project as a fun way to study measurement, symmetry, division, and fractions.

If, like Adina Popa—the International Ambassador for Loudoun County Public Schools, outside Washington, DC—you want your students to exchange multimedia book reviews, you can. Invite students to try out the ePals translator to learn greetings in the target language. Then have them research their partner country as an integral part of the exchange.[34]

Try sharing your own project on ePals. Invite others to partner with you!

Take Advantage of a Videoconferencing System

Use videoconferencing (via Skype, for example) to connect with other teachers who are interested in setting up a cultural exchange. If you're a foreign language teacher, try to connect with a teacher in another country who is interested in an exchange in which students communicate (at least some of the time) in the target language (English speakers speaking Spanish, and Spanish students speaking English, for example). Students will not only improve their foreign language skills, but will also come away with new relationships and rich insights into their partners' culture.[35]

Share a Favorite Book with Peers Halfway Around the World

Tap into the resources at the Global Reading Aloud Project to share books with others around the world.[36] This initiative gives students the opportunity to communicate and relate with peers through a combination of blogging and videoconferencing about a designated book. (Previous titles include *Tuck Everlasting* by Natalie Babbitt, and *Flat Stanley* by Jeff Brown.)

Involve Students in Collaborative Projects

Collaborative projects can focus on scientific or historical research, poetry, artwork, stories, artwork, essays, and cultural traditions with partner schools throughout the world. See the Global Virtual Classroom Clubhouse for ideas.[37]

How will you reach out to students and educators using telecommunications tool? If you are a teacher trainer, how will you support teachers in their global initiatives? Take a moment to sketch out your ideas using the questions in exhibit 6.1.

Jules advises Cross-cultural projects offer an ideal way for students to develop their "cultural competence" by helping them understand different nationalities and communities and their contributions to the world. These types of projects can also serve as a catalyst for students who are interested in learning more about their own racial and cultural roots.

Look for opportunities to help students connect their experiences with the larger world. They might write essays about the causes they care about (e.g., saving endangered species), exchange self-portraits and "day in the life of" journals with peers in other countries, and view historical events from multiple perspectives.[38]

Chad Detloff, Director of Global Opportunities in a California school, for example, helped arrange an exchange between students in his school and their peers in Korea. Students in both countries shared their responses to popular books—J. K. Rowling's Harry Potter series and Jeff Kinney's Diary of a Wimpy Kid series.

"It's not just about food, flags, maps, or the need to send kids to other countries," Detloff says. "A global citizen is one who sees the world from multiple perspectives. He or she knows that these are my views based on my values, but the person next to me is coming from a different place. From his or her perspective, it looks different."[39]

Another teacher, Lillie Marshall at Boston Latin Academy, taught in Ghana for a year—an experience that completely opened up her worldview. Now back in Boston, Marshall is passionate about helping her students cross boundaries as they learn to negotiate the cultural enclaves right in their own backyards.

Teaching in Ghana also convinced Marshall of the value of human stories about what life is like in other places. She had her students in Ghana write memoirs as part of a cultural exchange with her current class. "If kids get a global perspective it can enable huge behavior shifts. A lot of the negative behavior comes from the space they're in," she says. "Global education, if it can be done with a jolt, can be really effective. If kids can see the world and how people live, they will be less likely to make ill-informed comments."[40]

MOVING ONWARD AND UPWARD

Okay. You're all set to go. But what if you don't have access to the tools you need to become a more pioneering TechnoTeacher? In chapter 7, we show you how being brassy can serve you well as you beg, borrow, or simply ask for the tools you need to hone your practice and positively impact student learning.

EXHIBIT 6.1   **TechnoTeaching Action Plan**

Create a TechnoTeacher Action Plan as part of your blueprint for the year. Use these questions as a catalyst and jot down your ideas.

1. **Which online groups would be a good match for your interests?** Check around. Read a few of the discussion threads to pick up the vibe of the group. Target one or two groups where you, over time, might begin to feel at home. Sign up today.

2. **What will be the focus of your networking?** What do you want to learn from others? What do you plan to contribute? As with the three TechnoTeachers, you need to have a clear goal in mind. That way, you will feel productive and will be more likely to follow through.

3. **How much time can you spare to participate in your online communities each week?** Can you manage fifteen minutes every Tuesday and Thursday during planning time? Or a half-hour once a week after school? Figure out what works best for you and protect the time by entering it into your calendar. Be realistic so your goal doesn't become a burden. Remember, spending even just twenty minutes a week, if you do so consistently, could lead to fascinating results.

4. **Do you feel ready to have your students take on a global project?** If so, is there another teacher you can team up with? Is there a way to get parents involved?

5. **Are you willing to share your online life with colleagues?** Think about organizing a lunchtime workshop, for example, and invite fellow teachers who are interested in making global connections. Your hook can be a promise to share a few of your exchanges with teachers you have met virtually. What type of reciprocal learning took place? What problems and dilemmas did these educators help you address?

CHAPTER 7

Getting the
EdTech Tools You Need

You have now planned your Stellar Units and evaluated them. You have tried a few Dare Devil Missions and analyzed their impact on student learning. You have considered, and even experimented with, how you can work with others on a global scale. So you might be wondering what comes next—or, more likely, you are thinking *when can I do all the things I want to do*?

We often hear teachers say that one of the biggest barriers they face is a lack of time. We also hear that the biggest boon for a busy educator is *resources*—mainly because they can save time. A resource can be a simple work sheet or another human being. A resource can also be this book.

In this chapter, we analyze how you can create a budget, work out what you need, and even "dare" yourself to ask for resources from others. We also point you to free and low-cost materials and ideas available through the Internet.

If you are reading this chapter as a school leader or teacher professional developer, you may find information that you can use as the basis of a workshop or in a faculty meeting setting.

SKILLS & TOOLS IN DEPTH

Thus far, we have focused on a mixture of Skills & Tools (tackling new technologies and working out how you can up-skill yourselves and/or your classes), Content (Stellar Units and the year ahead), and Mindset (taking on Dare Devil Missions and other short-term projects).

Now it is time for a detailed look at how you can improve your toolkit and resources (otherwise known as the "things" that help you show off and/or use your Skills & Tools to help all children learn). As you know, we are not providing a "dummies" guide to using technology. We do not think you are a "dummy." You are a TechnoTeacher. You can find a tutorial online if you want to learn how to create a website; you can attend a workshop on apps if you want to learn how to select and download the best ones for your school.

Our goal is to teach you how to improve upon the tools you already have and how to add to your collection. Learning how to do this is harder than getting a whole new one-size-fits-all commercial program. It requires more ingenuity, but also offers greater rewards. In this chapter, we offer several tips in a range of categories:

- Working within your budget and learning how to supplement it
- Redesigning your TechnoTeaching classroom and other available spaces
- Reaching out to the school community (e.g., engaging parents, appealing to local businesses, borrowing equipment, working with departments of education) and big business
- Leveraging mentors and interns or existing student resources
- Financing and securing additional resources
- Planning a budget in nine simple steps
- Applying for a grant and other funding sources to get the tools you need

So let's get to it.

WHERE TO BEGIN?

Having taught mainly in low-income communities, we have spent a good deal of time trying to find the best materials at little or no cost. Where will you start? What will you do? How do you get your hands on what you need?

Jules has written grant proposals to fund summer literacy programs for struggling readers and writers in an underserved community in Boston. Principals have asked her to write mini-grants for materials to support literacy and new technologies. (She's also been on the other side of the equation, saying yes to pro bono work with school districts that are interested in upgrading their literacy and technology programs. School leaders can be very persuasive.)

Nic has personally resourced computer suites in several schools from scratch (begging and borrowing, but not stealing) and established multimedia curriculum spaces within school buildings (for large secondary schools). She has advised local authorities and regions in the U.K. on their use of technology in education, and now provides online help for teachers. She has also worked on the other side, by helping technology firms understand what teachers need. Rather than asking educators to work with what already exists, she has considered what *could be* out there in the classroom—a big difference. For example, when working with a smartphone in 2005, she was interested to see how students and teachers could share photographs using mobile technology when, at the time, cell phones were mainly viewed as texting-only devices. (Of course, nearly a decade later, TechnoTeachers are able to share photos on smartphones with much more ease and sophistication than she could have imagined back then.)

YOUR BUDGET AND OTHER FINANCIAL CONSIDERATIONS

Here is where you can begin planning your budget. Once you have your cohort, class, and Stellar Unit identified, zero in on the skills you need to improve. Then consider the practicalities. In schools, this normally comes down to money. These questions will help you start figuring out your finances:

- What funds do you have to work with?
- What is your new, or projected, budget for next year?
- What resources are currently available in your school?

Answering these questions might take some investigation. There are several things you can do to help identify the resources your school already has and learn how to maximize their capabilities.

Determining What Resources You Will Need

Begin by deciding which tools are necessities and which are luxuries from the following list.

- *Access to a suite of computers* (tablets, laptops, or desktops) is always helpful. This type of suite could be inside your classroom, in the library, or in another "bookable" room. It could also consist of a suite of laptops designated for your department area.
- *Wireless access* is great for a class on the move. Some schools will allow cell phone use (and therefore use of the Internet on students' personal devices).
- *A printer* for students' work or the capacity to create digital portfolios of work. Projects such as those we describe can be supported on many blogs or websites for nominal fees. To move forward, you will need support from the IT technicians in your school as well as your leadership team.
- *Recording equipment* can mean anything from a still camera or video camcorder to an editing suite and blue-screen material. Any one of these tools can be a bonus for multimedia projects.

But how can you obtain these tools? And how can you do it on a budget, whether you are a teacher or a school leader?

Jules advises Many schools have a range of available technology that ends up in a closet—underutilized, or even worse, never seeing the light of day. Although you may know some of the *hiding places, some gadgets may be hidden, still in boxes perhaps. We know teachers who have uncovered small treasures such as "talking pens," which enable students to record homework and then share their recordings with parents. Some have found hand-held devices that can help students who struggle with spelling, as well as foreign language software.*

The best thing to do is look. Speak to school leaders and IT specialists. Create an inventory of available tools and consider how you can put them to good use in your classroom.

Do not worry about whether you know how to use an interactive whiteboard or connect your iPad to the projector. Someone can always teach you (be it another staff member, a video tutor on YouTube, or a classmate in an edtech course). In fact, human capital may be your school's biggest asset. A member of your team, for example, may be a keen blogger or photographer and only too happy to help you.

In one of Nic's schools, for example, one of the English teachers used to be a professional photographer before she trained as an educator. Also, the head of geography's husband had done the lighting when touring with rock bands in the 1970s and was generous in lending a hand. Ask people about their talents in the staffroom. Take some cakes and invite people to talk about themselves. They may even want to become TechnoTeachers too.

Next, think about your classroom and the space available to you. You may need to request a different classroom assignment for the next academic year. Or perhaps you need to discuss your assignment with someone on the leadership team, to see what the arrangements are for next term. The point is to *ask and find out*.

Redesigning Your Classroom as a TechnoTeacher

In all of the schools Nic has taught in, she has given careful thought to her assigned space from a teaching and learning perspective. *What could that space be used for? What would they do in industry? What is the best way to go about making changes? What is in that closet?* She has also asked for permission to transform a textbook closet next to her classroom into an office, recording studio, or space for students to meet. If she can ask, so can you!

In one school, Nic discussed changing things around with the staff in her department area. They agreed. As a group they decided that, because they had adjoining classrooms and were teaching the same subjects, they could use the interior design to symbolize a more organized curriculum area. Nic then designated the two classrooms as the print room and the tech room.

The print room had large tables for project-based work and computers set up for desktop publishing. The tech room was then designed for audio and video editing, with as many sockets as could fit, and a cabinet that became a lockable, charging site. The trick was sitting back and considering the function of the rooms, and then designing the space around them just as you might a kitchen or a bedroom.

Similarly, the department began to reconsider the impact of color in the rooms. As recent homebuyers, Nic and one of her colleagues knew what a new coat of paint could do, and that by brightening a room, they could lift the "mood" of the space for its inhabitants. Accordingly, they painted both of the media rooms turquoise instead of the usual "classroom cream." This change created a cool—in all senses of the word—feel to the rooms. Through the use of color, people were able to see immediately that the space was a unified curriculum area. Just by asking others and being brave, Nic and her department were able to make quick, inexpensive changes that had a real impact on both teaching and learning. Could you do this at your school? What colors are your walls? Is your space flexible and functional?

Nic has also participated in building discussions. This is a step up from changing wall colors, but again, just by asking to be involved, she was. In the tech room, for example, she asked how many sockets *could* go around the room and how to arrange benching around them.

After the space was revamped, students were able to use a desktop computer while charging the camcorder they were using to download files, because there were enough sockets for each workstation. In other rooms, there were barely enough sockets for the computers, let alone for the staff laptop, printer, and so on. Once the room had the right number and proper placement of sockets, students were able to charge computers, camcorders, and cameras *as they worked.* That proved to be a real time saver when it came to working with the next class, because the equipment was prepared in advance. Again, by pausing to reflect on how they wanted to work, the teachers were able to create a space that supported them.

Take time to ponder what does and does not work for you. Consider what changes you need to implement to improve your teaching environment and make it more efficient.

Here are several ideas that Nic has tried out in various schools where she's taught. Try adapting one or two of them for your situation.

- Set off an area of the room as the "creative zone" (with beanbag chairs or a preloved sofa) for students to talk over their projects. You could also designate a "production zone," with computers and desks for student portfolio work.
- Turn wall space into personal pinboards where students and/or groups can pin up images, storyboards, and quotations to help with their work.
- Designate "clothesline" (washing line) areas for timelines or "power words."
- Change the seating arrangement to ensure that technology is easy to use.
- See if the maintenance or site team can add more sockets into the flooring under the desks so that students can charge laptops while working in groups. Or perhaps they could put benches or tabletops along the walls to give students additional workspace for desktop computers, as mentioned previously.
- Try removing the desk in your classroom (if you only need a stand for your laptop). Use the same space as the students, sitting at their tables with them. Or try working in that resource closet we discussed, which can become your mini-office and/or a secure space for hardware.

By redesigning your room—whether with a big budget or on a shoestring— you will start to see the classroom in a new way. And so will your learners.

Reaching Out to the School Community

Other contacts in the school community might be able to help you introduce additional computers and/or other gadgets into your classroom. Potential allies can include parents (through Parent Teacher Organizations), governors (in the U.K.), local businesses, and the local council. We've outlined a few approaches you might try.

Enlist parents

Parents can be your best allies when it comes to helping students engage with academics at all stages of schooling—yes, even in the case of adolescents. Nic has found that teachers often forget that parents have a wealth of information on their (own!) children and that they can be your best partners in improv- ing students' attitudes toward learning. At the same time, Jules has found that although many parents want to get involved, they are not sure how to go about it. You can show them exactly how they can have the most impact.

Start by inviting parents to visit your classroom. A dad who is a web designer or a mum who teaches a photography class at the local college can be powerful role models for your students. They can also share insider knowledge and skills related to their fields.

Be sure to let parents know about your upcoming instructional units and how they can get involved. Reassure them that you have considered the dan- gerous aspects of using digital tools (e.g., online predators) and explain the safeguards you have put in place.

Reach out to the small business community

Companies are able to "refresh" their technology (which means buying new computers and printers), and they may be delighted to donate their slightly outdated tools to your school (i.e., you).

You can also create relationships with local shops. If you have a camera center or computer outlet shop nearby, for example, befriend the manager and see what he or she can do for your students. Many merchants have links with headquarters, but are encouraged to act as independent stores. If the merchant is willing to offer a 10 percent discount, for example, or throw in a few extras for the school, those savings can really help. Additionally, the shop may be able to provide your students with work experience. You can repay the manager by suggesting reliable summer staff (students) for future hires.

Borrow equipment and/or space from outside the school site

Many companies, such as Apple, have loan schemes. Perhaps a local business would be willing to lend you equipment. If so, you will not have to invest in equipment, but just borrow digital tools for projects. Once your school sees how well this arrangement works, it may find a way to buy the technology for you to use with students.

Similarly, a recording studio might be able to give you a room for a day as long as you publicize its gift in the local newspaper and the students spread the word to their parents. Plan in advance and get the team involved.

Contact the school district

As part of the school community, the local school district may also be able to help. In the U.K., Nic worked with Southampton City Council and bought Sony Portable PlayStations (PSPs) for teachers to use with their classes. The PSPs were bookable (in class sets of thirty devices) across all schools in our area. In return, teachers reported back to Sony on the benefits of using these devices in different lessons. Overall, teachers were able to offer valuable insights, such as the fact that not all mathematics apps work with the curriculum, and some pieces of software are more bells and whistles than learning materials.

Speak to the education department in your school

Check with the education department for your school. See how far the budget can stretch to support your team's TechnoTeaching blueprint for the year. You could also find out if the department or school district has any technology not in use (e.g., a discarded printer or extra flash drives). Or volunteer to help launch an initiative for all the schools. Reach out to the community at large. It is always worth asking.

Fill your classroom for free

In the U.K., there is currently a huge resurgence in "filling your home for free." This initiative involves getting preloved furniture from yard sales (house clearances), "dumpster diving" ("skip scavenging" in the U.K.), or "freecycling" websites (which are now available in regions all over the English-speaking world). Instead of paying for furniture, you can see what people don't want, and give these finds a home. Just by looking on eBay, Craigslist, and other auction sites, you can find furniture for a small percentage of what you would pay in the store. You may need to repaint or reupholster chairs or sofas, but with a wealth of online tutorials (from YouTube to Pinterest) and DIY stores (with bargain buckets and great deals if you visit often enough), there really is no excuse anymore not to have a comfortable, workable home.

Have you considered applying this interior design strategy to your classroom? You can find cheap sofas for the corner of your classroom, whip up some beanbag chairs for story time, or find more chalkboard paint than you know what to do with. Dare yourself to furnish your classroom for free—as well as your living space at home!

Partnering with Big Business

To continue working with bodies beyond the school, you might check around in your community and see if there are any blue chip companies that would love to help your school, especially if you offer to work with their public relations team on writing an educational press release.

Nic advises   There are a number of ways that you can work with big businesses. First, be business-like. Ring up and schedule a meeting. Get a foot in the door. Then, don't be proud about enlisting other teachers and asking for support. Think of the children.

Ask the company if there is anything the school can help with regarding its young target audience or how its products are

> *represented to this market (or to parents). In the past I worked with a major international mobile phone contractor that wanted to portray the combination of cell phones plus teenagers in a positive light. The company wanted to distance itself from the U.K. craze of "happy slapping" (a form of bullying in which youths filmed their friends slapping unknowing victims in the face, and then uploaded the videos to YouTube).*
>
> *The company gave us thirty free cell phones with cameras for students to use in lessons. All we had to do was help with a press release afterward.*
>
> *I have also worked with Sony. We tried out a way for my students to review its new 3D screens; in turn Sony offered learning mentors to our bright but lively students. Students' mentors gave them insight into the industry, which helped them relate to life beyond the classroom.*
>
> *In many cases, you just have to ask.*

A business, software company, or bank may have its headquarters near your school and be happy to help, as long as you are willing to be included in one of its press releases. It could mean that you provide a "student testing" group for the organization. In exchange, it might invite your students for internships ("work experience" in the U.K.) and/or provide technology mentors.

If there is a school event coming up, and you know of a technology giant near you, contact the main office and see what you can accomplish by joining forces. Do some research and find the name of someone who might be interested in working with you. Call that person and set up a meeting to see what you can do. Be sure to keep the dialogue going after the meeting. It will be up to you to push this agenda. Make it clear that the company will not only be helping students, but that the students will also be helping it in return.

Recruiting Interns and Mentors

Others in your school, such as interns and mentors, might be willing to get involved with a project (the redesign of your classroom, for example). In exchange, your students can provide these adults with a fresh, young perspective on the projects they are involved in.

Leveraging Student Resources

Although it means that you will have to address your school's policy on cell phones, think about the fact that many students have a decent camera sitting in their pocket most days. This means they can take images and film videos for coursework or projects, without your needing to worry about storing school equipment. Students can then e-mail you their projects (if they have a smartphone) or upload them directly to YouTube or to their blogs.

SECURING ADDITIONAL RESOURCES

There are several more things you can do to obtain additional resources. It is best to create a business plan and be as professional as possible. Do not discuss this idea in the corridors. Do create a proposal and book a few meetings. Create an agenda. Allow time to be focused and purposeful. The administrative/ strategic side of this may be new to many of you outside of management, but it is straightforward if you follow a few rules.

Framing Your Budget and Student Outcomes

First, you'll need to create and justify a budget. Anyone who has to fill in budget forms should also be able to defend them. The school (or the principal) will want to hear how you have saved money and how students have progressed as a result of the investment. Regardless of what subject you teach, the two top ways to frame your discussion are *value for money* and *impact on learning*. If you want the school to create a new television studio, be ready to explain how students will get better grades in social studies or become better writers as a result. (Also point out how you will be able to save money by procuring the tech tools from the particular vendor you suggest.)

Deciding What You Really Want

Next you need to consider what you want and how much it will cost. Do you want some new software or hardware? What are the alternatives? Are they free? Do you want industry standard, or something to last several years? Do you need brand new, or will old-but-working be fine? Do you need to include a full- or part-time technician as a resource? All of these questions will have a bearing on how much money you will need.

Focusing on the Big Picture

You may be able to get most of the resources you need from your principal. Or perhaps another member of the administration or leadership team has a little pot of gold just ready for you to use. The chances are slim, though. Your principal may be as excited as you about your vision—or not. You need to judge your response accordingly and ensure that you keep everyone on your side. Overall, your objective is to get your hands on money for your students that might be spent elsewhere.

If you are creating a school budget, the highest-level administrator will be the one to sign off on it. There may be senior-level team members acting as gatekeepers, but ultimately you will need to speak to the person at the top of the ladder. Be a bit savvy here. If you know that the school doesn't have money, do some research on what grants are available and when the proposals are due (more on grant writing later in this chapter). Also find out what local businesses can add to the equation so you will know what the balance is—then ask for just that amount.

Show how passionate you are and how much planning you have done on your own.

Conducting Field Research

Find out whether any local schools are using the technology tools you have in mind and, if so, go visit them. Ask teachers how edtech has supported teaching and learning and whether there has been a positive impact on student learning. Discuss the process school staff went through in turning their vision into a reality.

Ask school staff how they conduct parent evenings with the principal. You can boost a school's local reputation by showing parents around a new, shiny technology lab, introducing a contemporary course, or even screening a film students have created about their school.

WRITING A GRANT PROPOSAL

Going after grant funding can be a big commitment. It can also be a leadership opportunity because of all there is to do, including locating the funding source, assembling a team, delegating responsibility, and submitting your proposal. Others who have a deep knowledge of the grant funding world and how things work can point you in the right direction so you can get your projects noticed—and funded.

If you live in the United States, you might find the following resources helpful.

- *eSchool News Funding Center.* This site lists up-to-the-minute opportunities.[1]
- *Fundraising and Grant Resources for Tech Integration.* George Lucas's Foundation, Edutopia, has gathered resources for you at this site.[2]
- *Writing a Successful Grant Proposal.* On this site, experts guide you through the grant writing process.[3]
- *Grants4Teachers.* Browse this site to get a sense of the types of projects that are being funded. Maybe there's a good match for you.[4]

The following sites might be helpful for readers in Europe.

- *British Council and Department for Education.* This comprehensive website includes well-organized information about funding and support for schools.[5]

- *EU Comenius Funding.* This site provides funding opportunities for language teachers to receive training for one to four weeks in a country other than the one in which they work.[6]
- *British Council's Connecting Classrooms.* If your school is involved in a partnership between the U.K. and another country, this site will support visits by you and your teaching partner.[7]
- *eTwinning.* This site comprises an online community and collaboration tools for schools in any of thirty-two European countries.[8]

Get together a group of teachers who have a particular project in mind and give it a try.

CARING AND SHARING RESOURCES

If other members of your school staff feel they would also benefit from a new suite of tablets or cameras, you could work together to create a "whole school" set of resources. Consider where the equipment you purchase would be locked as well as how it would be signed out. Also think about which curricular areas and out-of-school clubs would be interested in sharing your new tools.

Nic advises   Here are four key tips for securing TechnoTeaching resources:

- **Ask for more than you need.** Why not? If you want stop-motion camera facilities or a blue screen so you can film news reports, go for it. Many universities (and schools) are now using these resources, and there is no reason why students in your school shouldn't also be using them.

- *Ensure that all the information in your proposal is well thought out.* You need to consider the logistics of your classroom from all angles, so you are not trying, for example, to screen films next to a non-soundproofed music room. You must also have the correct amount of workstations for students, so that three seventeen-year-old boys are not crammed next to each other for a two-hour lesson. The key is to make sure that you are able to move around the room and students can work on any number of projects independently.
- *Plan for all areas, including consumable supplies like flash drives and microphones.* Think about how long you want the project to last, and what this means in terms of resources. You may aim to get three years of materials, especially if you think that you might not get any more money after this round. Better yet, ask to have funds allocated in stages rather than in a lump sum.
- *Be positive, patient, and calm.* Wait and smile. Remember that this initiative might be more important to you than it is to others. It also may take time to get your proposal ready. And although you may want to get started straightaway, the administration may need to call several meetings (over several weeks).

NINE SIMPLE STEPS FOR PLANNING A BUDGET PROPOSAL

It is best to get your resources before you start a new program, course, or initiative. If your school is keen to support you with TechnoTeaching as part of your continuing professional development, it is worth discussing how far that support will reach. If you are improving your skills as a personal choice, there is no reason why the school shouldn't support you, as you will also be improving the learning experience for your students.

The budget Nic has devised for you breaks down into nine different areas.

1. *Breakdown of major specific expenditure.* This category zeroes in on all the big, expensive items—a class set of cameras, some industry-standard editing software, or a few new computers, for example. Here, it is beneficial to think about how and how many students will use the technology tools. Will more students be added to the class in the future? If you do not deal with questions like these now, you will have to later on, when you don't have time for weighing the pros and cons.

2. *Consumable supplies.* Your consumables include all the supplies that will get used up quickly, including pens, folders, paper, and blank CD/DVDs and their cases. It is a good idea to add magazines (either subject- or age-specific) and other print material to your consumable list.

3. *Minor specific supplies.* Rechargeable batteries, external hard drives, USBs, and firewire cables all fall under this heading.

4. *Estimates of developments for the area (directive, department, year group).* Plan ahead. If you are starting with a low budget bid, add more funds so everyone will have at least the minimum of what they need to be effective TechnoTeachers. If you expect to receive funds up front, have a contingency plan for what might break, go missing, or need upgrading during the school year.

5. *Targets related to curriculum requirements.* This category, again, could include a part-time technician to free you up as your responsibility grows, or resources for a new room. It could mean bringing in new exams and/or courses or linking with other school areas, such as art and music. Be sure to include any specific targets or grade levels related to the budget (e.g., writing software for children in the early grades).

   If you are writing a proposal for the second year of a three- or five-year plan, be ready to demonstrate how these targets were met in year one and how you plan to build on them moving forward.

6. *Training for staff development.* Although your principal may have this base covered, it is always worth adding in training for yourself or other school staff. Extra funds would allow you to create additional stipends for school staff who take on more responsibilities.

   Training for staff development could also include a subscription to a particular website for further resources, admission to technology-in-education fairs, or courses.

   Also bear in mind excellent training opportunities that are low-cost or free. Apple runs free workshops for its software and hardware, for example. You might also check out meetups in your area where edtech types gather. Look for special interest groups (SIGs) for organizations such as the International Society for Technology Educators. Also sign up for webinars and seminars on a wealth of topics through EdWeb and TED Talks for Educators.[9]

7. *Digital equipment and accessories.* What will you need? If there is anything that you haven't included so far, do so now!

8. *DVDs, books, and subscriptions.* If you have access to YouTube, you may find that you don't need to buy many items in this category. If you are hoping to incorporate a new course or initiative while becoming a TechnoTeacher, think about the curriculum resources you will need. These might include subscription-based resource sites for your area, such as the U.S. site BrainPop and the U.K. site Edusites, which charge modest fees.[10] Remember to include these annual fees in your budget.

   In general, always ask yourself what is the best teaching resource and what is the most economical way to go, and remember to factor these expenses into the budget evaluation at the end of the year.

9. *Photocopying/art materials/stationery.* Include a line item for laminating or photocopying on colored or plain printer paper. Although (we hope) you will be using e-portfolios, your school may still require hard copies of the work, so be prepared.

Jules advises Nic has given you many ideas for gathering the resources you will need to realize your goals as a TechnoTeacher, based on her firsthand experiences.

In addition, I suggest taking a couple of minutes to jot down a few action items in your TechnoTeaching notebook while the question of funds and resources is fresh in your mind. For example:

- What resources are already available right now in your classroom or school?
- What additional tools do you need most of all so your students can write a graphic novel, create a photo journal, or film a video, for example?
- How will you reach out to parents for support?
- How will you reach out to the wider community for support, including applying for grants from foundations and other funding agencies?
- How will you reach out to big business for support?
- How will you and your students give back to the people and/or companies that have been generous to you?

FINAL THOUGHTS

We hope you now feel that you have the tools to improve your skills, mindset, and above all your ability to ensure that your students succeed as global learners. The new resources you gather will grease the skids for teaching your Stellar Units as well as help you flesh out your blueprint for the year ahead.

While this chapter has intentionally not been about the TechnoTeaching characters, you can imagine TechnoWhy? Melissa writing a grant proposal for a classroom set of tablets. And what about TechnoOK Zayid? Picture him developing a new working relationship with a blue chip company, one that wants to give back to the world by investing in education in developing nations. Meanwhile, TechnoYes! Jasmine is partnering with a software developer to make a killer app about history in the making, with help from her students.

But primarily, we wanted this chapter to be about *you*, the TechnoTeacher taking a creative approach to gathering all the resources you need. In the next chapter you will see how having the right resources, along with a well-designed space in which you and your students can be creative and productive, sets the stage for thinking deeply about your practice. While it is certainly a boon to have the right skills and tools in play, without a TechnoTeacher mindset it's nothing more than window dressing. We will show you how to think deeply about your practice—how to use the x-ray vision teachers are so good at cultivating to get to the heart of the matter.

CHAPTER 8

Reflecting on the Year

N ow it is time for you to be a keen observer and a reflective practitioner, drawing upon your professional experience and intuition. In this chapter, we ask you to stand back and reflect on your goals, failures, and successes along the path to becoming a TechnoTeacher. Based on your insights, you can make a well-informed, realistic plan for next year.

Begin by circling back to the self-assessment you did in chapter 2 (specifically, exhibit 2.1). What did you learn about yourself early on in becoming a TechnoTeacher that served as a defining moment? Which top Stellar Units will you adopt as part of your repertoire? Which ones will you replace altogether with something that will make better use of (and stretch) your Skills & Tools, Content, and Mindset? What Dare Devil Missions and other short-term projects will you add next year? It's time to build a blueprint for the future while your experiences are fresh in your mind.

Do not fear. We will show you how.

DONALD SCHÖN AND PROFESSIONAL ARTISTRY

Let's give some thought to understanding and reflecting on your teaching styles and strategies—your "craft" if you like. Your craft is your *professional artistry*, in the words of Donald A. Schön, a major proponent of the reflective learning technique.

169

To Schön, the type of artistry good teachers exhibit "is a high-powered, esoteric variant of the more familiar sorts of competence all of us exhibit every day in countless acts of recognition, judgment, and skillful performance."[1] In fact, sometimes we don't even realize we're doing it; our artistry becomes the way we perform in the classroom or as school leaders.

JOHN DEWEY AND REFLECTIVE ACTION

Schön's theories about professional artistry are rooted in educational reformer John Dewey's philosophy about reflective practice. Dewey, in the early part of the twentieth century, distinguished between *routine action* and *reflective action*, a perspective that is still relevant today.[2] Routine action is that which is automatic, with few surprises: put an egg into a pan of water until it boils, turn off the flame, wait 2.5 minutes, and voilà, a perfect soft-boiled egg. According to Dewey, routine action is guided by "impulse, tradition, and authority."[3] Schools themselves are cultures in which routine actions take hold, from the management style of school leaders to the faculty's traditions for parent "open house" nights. Faculty members often work within this culture, seldom questioning their own big-picture goals—the deep-down beliefs that inspired them to become educators in the first place.

We suspect that as a TechnoTeacher you want to make omelettes rather than soft-boiled eggs (or soufflés, if you really like a challenge), and this is where reflective action comes in. According to Dewey, reflective action refers to "behavior which involves active, persistent, and careful consideration of a belief or practice in light of the grounds that support it and the further consequences to which it leads."[4]

In other words, Dewey believed we should be willing to recognize problems and go about solving them. For educators, reflective action involves being analytical about the sociocultural and political context in which they teach. Is their leadership team top-down or bottom-up, for example? Are students' parents high-powered professionals or newcomers to the country who feel somewhat marginalized by society? What languages do students speak at home and at school? Is the school situated in a liberal, moderate, or conservative community? These types of factors, and how they influence teaching and learning, are important to consider through reflective action.

A reflective teacher adopts these three attitudes, according to Dewey:

- *Open-mindedness:* Being receptive to ideas other than your own.
- *Responsibility:* Understanding that you are ultimately responsible for the consequences of your actions (e.g., the subtext of the subjects you teach and how students might respond to a "hidden curriculum").
- *Wholeheartedness:* Doing everything that you can to meet the needs of all students. This means making up your own mind—not being swayed by the beliefs and practices of those more powerful than you, hoping they'll reward you with good reviews or a coveted teaching assignment. Wholeheartedness means living up to your personal philosophies about education.[5]

Dewey believed all three qualities need to be in place before you can truly engage in *reflection*, which enables us to use foresight and develop a plan to achieve our goals.[6] Why not take a moment now to reflect on these three qualities?

You probably read the preceding list and either nodded or mentally agreed with the first two. Then you may have wobbled slightly with the third, as it is a "biggie." However, we want you to be honest with yourself and consider to what degree *you do everything that you can to meet the needs of all students.* Then weigh how much you *could do.*

THE REFLECTIVE PRACTITIONER

In his book *The Reflective Practitioner*, Schön takes several of Dewey's ideas and brings them into modern times. Schön saw the value of introspection for professionals in several fields, including teaching, that require artistry.

The Reflective Practitioner was required reading when Jules was in graduate school. Her reaction changed from *Who has time to be reflective? I have to grind my way through three semesters of statistics!* to *Why was I too blind to see that teaching at its core is an art form, and that it doesn't make a person flaky to say that out loud?* Being a good teacher involves so much more than factual information; it involves the ability to reflect in real time before making decisions that will impact a child for many years to come. Most problems are not straightforward like the ones you read about in textbooks; they have twists and turns and sharp corners that call for reflection not only in the moment, but throughout your entire career.[7]

Dewey believed that when we are puzzled about a student's behavior and what steps to take next, we are on the cusp of learning something new and important. Schön took this philosophy one step further, adding that "reflecting *after* you've [acted]" is also essential to developing your craft.[8] We have all had the experience, sometimes frustratingly, of seeing what we *should* have done in a tricky situation with 20/20 hindsight. This phenomenon reminds us of the French expression *Avoir l'espirit de l'escalier,* which literally means to have "the wit of the staircase." It refers to the inability to think of witty or intelligent comebacks until you are climbing the stairs and the moment has fled! Our work with children is more than finding witty comebacks, but we have all felt the sting of the missed opportunity. But we know as teachers there is always tomorrow. In a nutshell, this rueful backward glance marks the transition from *What did I do* to *What could I do next time?*

WHY BECOME A REFLECTIVE PRACTITIONER?

When teaching graduate students, Jules is sometimes surprised by their attitude toward refining their practice. Often she finds that her students, who had made a name for themselves back home, have enrolled in advanced classes *not* to have their world order shaken up, but to get validation for the teaching methods they are already using. Rather than reflecting on the theories and research they are reading about, and how they could use those insights when they return to the field, some students want to hear that what they are already doing is perfect exactly as is—no alterations, thank you.

Sadly, Nic has encountered a similar attitude in the U.K. as part of teacher training. She's met many teachers who feel that they are doing very well, that they know it all and have heard it all before, and that there really is nothing that they could improve on, as there is not enough time or resources. This is where it can get hard to defend your peers, but there are weak links in every chain/change. There are good teachers and those who are not well suited to this type of work. There are teachers who do not want to change and those who want to improve as much as they can. It is the latter group—these reflective teachers who are always striving to broaden their perspective, take more responsibility for their students, and be wholehearted in figuring out how to boost student learning—that we want to work with. Where do you feel that you sit on this spectrum? Since you are reading this book, our hunch is that you are already well ahead of the curve.

The rewards of open-mindedness, responsibility, and wholeheartedness can hardly be overstated. After all, teacher education programs, no matter how rigorous, cannot prepare you for the changing world we live in, or every type of teaching situation you might encounter. There will always be new challenges. As a reflective practitioner, you will be able to draw from everything you have learned, think critically about new situations (e.g., bullying, teaching children with disruptive behaviors), and apply what you know in novel ways.[9] Reflective teaching puts you in control, helping you go from reactive to proactive.[10]

Which brings us back to TechnoTeaching. It is impossible to learn everything you need to know about integrating new technologies in an undergraduate or graduate seminar, even if the course is taught by a wizard and you have state-of-the art digital tools to experiment with. Technology is changing too quickly to make this type of mastery realistic. And the abilities and sensibilities of children in the digital age are evolving along with it. It might help at this point to stop, step back, and see how our TechnoTeachers reflect upon their work.

OUR TECHNOTEACHERS AND THEIR REFLECTIVE ANALYSIS

We realize it may seem slightly improbable that all three of our TechnoTeachers have embraced global citizenship wholeheartedly in their first year of adapting our TechnoTeaching guide. It is a quantum leap. But remember, TechnoWhy? Melissa swims competitively, a state of mind that sometimes rubs off on her teaching. We also know that TechnoOK Zayid loves novelty and is bicultural (having emigrated from India to the U.K.). He is also raising two sons who are part of the digital age. And TechnoYes! Jasmine is the sort of idealistic person who thinks that if everyone takes a few small steps, we can change the world. So, yes, even though just a single year has elapsed, we ask you to suspend disbelief while we check in with our three energetic teachers in the late spring as they reflect on the past school year and plan for the future. Like you, they are starting to find themselves—and others—online more and more often.

Imagine the following scenarios.

TechnoWhy? Melissa's Self-Reflection

TechnoWhy? Melissa and her tech coordinator, Mimi, have just ordered dinner at an outdoor café overlooking Narragansett Bay. Mimi reviews the teaching notebook Melissa has been writing in this year, while Melissa checks e-mail on her new iPad (a birthday present from her husband).

"You've *really* come far this year," says Mimi. "You realize that, don't you?"

"Yes, I guess so. But I still feel like I have a lot of catching up to do."

"What unit from this past year would you say was most successful?" asks Mimi.

"Well . . . I guess the Stellar Unit on historical fiction. Kids learned so much by writing book reviews. And, let's face it, they always write better when it's for their peers," says Melissa. "Just like the research says."

"So. What's next?"

"I was thinking about your professional development session on digital citizenship.

About having kids step out of the terrarium we live in and find out about other cultures in the world," says Melissa.

"Like your 'Travel Broadens the Mind' unit this year?" Mimi asks. "I loved it when your students interviewed people who'd traveled to exotic places and then made a pitch to the class about visiting that country."

"It will build on that, but the focus will be on historical *fiction*. Fiction that goes along with my unit on the Revolutionary War. Maybe with a spotlight on the British perspective, using a poem or piece of artwork as a catalyst. I think for me the challenge would be more about Skills & Tools. More about how to link up globally, working with another teacher and class in another country, rather than Content. I would like to figure out how to make this . . . a normal way of working, just with another teacher in another classroom. Be a real twenty-first-century teacher."

The waiter arrives with two glasses of wine and a chilled platter of Wellfleet oysters. The iPad is put to one side.

"So a week or two ago I posted a message to Edmodo," says Melissa, "saying something along those lines."

"You did? I get it. Glad to see you're putting your competitive streak to good use," Mimi says.

Melissa begins to protest, then thinks better of it. "Maybe," she says, smiling and squeezing a lemon wedge over an oyster. "You might be right."

TechnoOK Zayid's Self-Reflection

Meanwhile, on another continent, TechnoOK Zayid sits in a corner of the local pub, laptop open. While his wife and sons are down at the beach, he finishes reflecting on the past year and his progress with TechnoTeaching with a cool pint of pale ale. He is ready to plan the year ahead.

Zayid's team teacher, Erik, stops by, as planned, to compare notes and grab a beer. Zayid goes to the bar to order a pint while Erik looks over his notes.

"You know, I'm just now realizing how much difficulty some of my students had with the historical context of the poetry," Zayid says, popping a fresh pint in front of Erik and sitting down. "They just don't get the fact that what people experience—then or now—has a real impact on the content. They get too bogged down in the literary devices and the use of commas. I've got to teach it much better next year—sort it out for them, be more inspiring—especially for my EALs." Zayid pauses a moment. "Hey, why we don't we teach a unit together? Maybe a cross-cultural exchange based on a poem's historical context. Same time, different countries, same ideas, different poems? What do you think?"

"Yeah, sounds good," says Erik. "My kids seem to be mostly engaged with the texts—they don't seem to grasp that the context is also important. They think they can just Google it rather than try to imagine what it was like in the 1780s. They just need to understand a few facts about the time, really. What about a documentary-style project about the eighteenth century? Something to do with video? That seems to get them focused."

"We could. And maybe something with William Blake—since we're supposed to cover that unit anyway . . . I ran out of time this year, though. I really didn't spend as much time on it as I should have," Zayid says.

"Hm. That might work. We could get them to research the facts of what life was like then, compared with now, and do something with video. That could be the 'bait' and then we could relate it to Blake's poems? That would be a nice way to kick off the new term," Erik replies.

"Maybe we could connect with a school somewhere cool—maybe on the continent. Or really push it and go global? Like New Zealand? Or America? Or Canada, and not *just for* the hockey. Yeah . . . something like a spelling bee—swapping facts instead of doing spellings though," Zayid drums out a jazz riff on the table with his pencil.

Erik takes a sip and smiles. "I'm picturing California. Los Angeles. Palm trees. Roller boots. The beach . . . A school exchange trip for the teachers—I mean students! Ha! You ought to post a message on Edmodo. There must be something we can overlap on," he says.

"I already did, a couple of weeks ago. It's in the hands of the fates."

"How'd you know I'd agree?"

"Just a hunch," Zayid grins. "Don't pack your bags just yet."

TechnoYes! Jasmine's Self-Reflection

Meanwhile in Québec City, TechnoYes! Jasmine meets with Misha, a first-year social studies teacher on her team. They meet in the teachers' lounge where Jasmine is poring over her journal (yes, paper), which is crammed with complicated asides to herself, sticky notes, and student writing. She pulls out her TechnoTeaching self-reflection sheet and begins writing.

"What do *you* think was one of our best projects from the past year?" Jasmine asks.

"The keypal exchange with Claudia. Hands down," says Misha, as he reaches into his backpack and pulls out two bottles of iced tea and a bunch of grapes.

"Hmmm." Jasmine writes a few notes. "The class really did enjoy connecting with other kids in Brazil," she agrees. "Remember how quickly they learned a few expressions in Portuguese?"

"*Ooh, sim, eu.* And being 'digital citizens.' Don't forget that," says Misha.

"Right. The computer project turned out to be the perfect way to cap off the keypal exchanges. Especially for students who have behavior issues. When they got to help other kids and be the experts, their attitude was much, *much* better."

"It was great to see them in action," Misha nods. "But you can't start with that unit in the fall, right? It's too advanced. You'd have to work up to it."

"Good thinking. But what if I told you I already posted a message last night to see if there's any interest out there? I was thinking of setting up the links now to start next spring."

"Any takers?"

"Not yet. But hopefully someone in another time zone will read it later. You never know, right? I might even ask Claudia if she will do it again, or if she has any peers who might like to get involved."

Jasmine fires up her laptop, reaches for a handful of grapes, and starts making notes.

REFLECTING ON YOUR YEAR

Now that you've seen our TechnoTeachers' approaches to reflective analysis, it's time to begin your own evaluation of the past year. We'll offer tips to get you started.

Nic advises *Before you start the evaluation process, remember not to be too hard on yourself. It might be that you have started to use a new website or have gained a little extra confidence. Give yourself credit for all the times you have shown initiative.*

Think of the unmeasurable factors like student engagement, improved relationships within your classroom, and attitude toward teaching. These factors are at least as important as progress points, new IT equipment, and attendance figures. After all, teaching is a combination of hard and soft skills.

Be sure to reflect on all aspects of this journey, even if it feels a little silly or uncomfortable. The odds are that these soft skills will be the elements that are more emotional (more personal); they have the potential to improve your reputation and even your school culture.

Solicit Student Feedback

To kick off your review of your impact in the classroom, go directly to the source: your students. They are your audience. You may have an idea of what you wanted them to learn from your lessons, but they are the ones who can tell you just how successful (or not) you were and are.

Begin by taking a moment to review your blueprint for Stellar Units, Dare Devil Missions, seasonal/monthly projects, or your global activities. List several titles on the board and ask students for their opinions. *What did you enjoy learning about the most? Why was that? What would you like to do following this? How would you explain this to another student? What would you do if you were teaching this?* While you may think you know what they got out of various units, students might have quite a different take. Their views, if you are ready to hear them, may offer a few surprises that you can put to use next time.

Write It Down

Using the self-reflection questions in table 8.1, meet with one or more colleagues and start writing. Or, if you prefer, take turns interviewing each other and jotting down ideas. In either case, this activity will help you carry out a detailed self-assessment and learn more about how your colleagues approach their work. If you are an administrator or teacher professional developer, the self-evaluation process can provide a terrific opportunity for you to help school staff reach the next level.

PLANNING YOUR FUTURE AS A TECHNOTEACHER

Now that you have taken a close look at where you have been, it is time to write down your ideas for how you will continue to improve your own practice going forward.

Jules advises   You could use several different data collection methods to help you advance as both a TechnoTeacher and as a reflective practitioner.

You can begin with a journal of your experiences (like TechnoYes! Jasmine), as mentioned in chapter 3. The journal can be one that you keep in your computer bag or a digital file. Use it to record significant learning experiences for you and your students, track your self-development as an educator, and inspire conversations with colleagues.

TABLE 8.1 **TechnoTeaching self-reflection guide**

TechnoTeaching framework	What were my goals in this area?	How did I make progress (identify unit)?	What were my successes?	What were my challenges?	What are my goals for next year?
Skills & Tools: Used a variety of edtech and other digital tools and learned new ones with ease.					
Skills & Tools: Accessed resources and support systems that helped me acquire the necessary skills and tools.					
Content: Integrated technology in a deliberate manner and to meet the needs of all learners.					
Content: Engaged students in the curriculum in ways that would not be possible otherwise.					
Mindset: Embraced the use of technology and was willing to take risks.					
Mindset: Engaged in continuous learning and reflection.					
Mindset: Worked to ensure that students were prepared appropriately to assume their roles as global citizens.					

You will be surprised by what you can learn just from taking the time to jot down your ideas in the moment and then reviewing them later when you have gained more perspective. As educator Jack C. Richards said: "Reflective teaching suggests that experience alone is insufficient for professional growth, but that experience coupled with reflection can be a powerful impetus for teacher development."[11]

Another idea is to videotape one of your lessons. You can set up the camcorder and do it yourself. Or you and a colleague can take turns videotaping each other and discussing your lessons (what you hoped to accomplish, how it went, and what you might do differently next time).

Last, get involved with a coaching program that pairs novices with experienced edtech teachers to provide each other with mentoring, exchange how-to's, and, in effect, become each other's life rafts. If your school doesn't have a coaching program, you can always get together with other faculty members and start one. Why not?

Determine Your Top Priorities for Next Year

Look at the list of goals in table 8.1 and prioritize your top five for the upcoming academic year. This could be based upon a conversation with your performance manager, your students' feedback, your own thoughts, or a combination.

Create a Blueprint for Next Year

In designing your plan for TechnoTeaching next year, begin by setting concrete daily, weekly, and monthly goals.

Is one of your goals to meet with coteachers more often to evaluate progress? If so, write it down. Have you been meaning to build your skill set to teach a unit that will involve video production? Fit it in. Do you need eight weeks, not six, to teach a Stellar Unit? Map it out using the templates for first and second semester.

How does your blueprint look? Exciting? Daunting? Manageable? Talk it over with colleagues (e.g., your school leaders or team teachers) who have a stake in your success. Ask for advice. Suggest pooling resources. No one person can do it all regardless of how it plays out in Hollywood movies. (It took two of us to write this book, after all.)

OUR TECHNOTEACHERS PLAN FOR THE FUTURE—TOGETHER

Once again, we ask you to suspend disbelief as you read about our three TechnoTeaching archetypes and the messages they received after writing to other educators all over the world. Imagine the following scenarios.

As the sun sinks into the bay, TechnoWhy? Melissa and Mimi abandon the gooey remains of a brownie with chocolate sauce and get ready to leave the restaurant. As they wait for the bill to arrive, Melissa checks her iPad to see if she has any takers on the message she posted to Edmodo (about collaborating on a cross-cultural project based on historical fiction). While Mimi is busy taking a photo of sailboats, Melissa realizes how excited she is about making this connection.

Her iCloud opens and—yes!—there is a new message in her inbox from a teacher in England.

Hi there, Melissa. What about the two of us looking at different important periods of time in our own countries—think you mentioned the Revolution? I am looking at William Blake and *The Songs of Innocence and Experience* with my class (published in 1789—that's just a few years after the War ended, right?), so perhaps I could get them to think about England in the 1780s, and might even see if I can link up with some museums over here. I figure I could beg a historian mate to get involved—might be able to help you too? What do you think?

> Maybe a "poetry slam" about the American Revolution could be a good vehicle for this. My pupils have been doing these in English lessons here and love them! My plan was to have them research facts online, rope in some videoconference speakers, and get them to create poems before the slam.
>
> Would this work well in your country? Perhaps involving some sort of multimedia project? We could film the slams and get the opposite class to judge them. What do you think? –Zayid

"Hey, Mimi. Someone's read my message. A guy from England," says Melissa. "He sounds very creative. I'll just send a quick reply."

> Good to hear from you, Zayid. Very interested. It's getting late here, but let's try to work out the details via Skype or e-mail tomorrow if you have any free time. Really interested in hearing more.
> Kindest regards,
> Melissa

TechnoYes! Jasmine and Misha finish evaluating the past school year and create a Google Doc about ideas for next year as a work in progress. Jasmine checks her e-mail before shutting down. "You won't believe this," she says.

She tells Misha that a secondary high school teacher from Rhode Island has responded to her message about joining forces, this time on another Skype in the Classroom project. It is similar to the one Jasmine did last year about computers in Brazil. *Ping.* Another message appears on her screen. This one from England. Same thing. "Wow," Jasmine says. "That was fast."

A month later, TechnoOK Zayid is busy setting up his classroom. *Ping.* A message from a teacher in Canada appears on his phone. It is a thread on one of the LinkedIn message boards. He stops marking the classbooks and opens the message. It reads:

> Hi Global Teacher!
> Would you be interested in helping students in Brazil who live in poor areas? I've seen a video on TED Talks for Educators and was inspired. My elementary students and I are from Canada. We want to connect more globally and are very interested in helping less advantaged students gain access to computers and then learn how to use them once they have them. Students love being the experts and offering advice.
> I wasn't sure if you would be interested, but thought it was worth a go!
> —Jasmine (writing from Québec City)

"Hmmm," says Zayid to himself. "Wonder if that will be hard work? Their kids are younger, but I think we could still help . . . Actually, it would give the weaker students in my classes some confidence. Yes, I think the students would love it, and I know my boss would too! I'm going to do it."

> Greetings, Jasmine in Canada. Yes! Count me in. –Zayid, from the U.K.

A week later, another *ping* in Zayid's inbox. The teacher he wrote to in America (Melissa) wants to talk brass tacks about an "X the Pond" poetry slam. *I'm suddenly quite the popular bloke*, he chuckles to himself.

> Hi Mel,
> Well, I was thinking that I might even see if the English department wants to get involved too. By doing what? What do you think? Would that work at your end too? Maybe we could get the whole-year group involved— or the school? Is that too much? Maybe one step at a time, eh?!
> The world certainly is shrinking, isn't it, Mel? I hope I can keep up with you on the tech side of things!
> Best regards,
> Zayid (from Bournemouth, England)

Melissa looks up Bournemouth on Google Maps.

Hello Zayid,

Oh, I'm pretty sure you'll be able to keep up with me. I'm just getting started. It's my students you have to worry about. They're the advanced ones. I am the one learning now. They are now calling me "pre-WWW" (World Wide Web), in a *hopefully* affectionate way!

Looking forward to starting a new WWW adventure with you soon.

—Melissa (from the "Ocean State")

TechnoTeaching Manifesto

The following is our TechnoTeaching Manifesto—a summary of core values and ways to re-envision your practice.

- *Be bold.* *Be a dare devil*—no matter where you are on the TechnoTeaching continuum.
- *Build on what you know and care about.* The subject matter you know and are passionate about provides you with the best way to begin your TechnoTeaching journey (i.e., designing your Stellar Units).
- *Plan ahead.* Not simply planning for the next unit, but mapping everything out for an entire school year (i.e., creating a TechnoTeaching blueprint) will reward your time and effort tenfold.
- *Create a support system.* While it is great to have cool gadgets and goodies at your fingertips, your best resource is human capital—the educators you have access to, near and far, who can become part of your support system, with you giving back by sharing what you have learned (yes, even the disasters).
- *Think globally.* Children growing up in the digital age (whether we call them Generation Zs, digital natives, or millennials) are living in a vastly different world than the one in which we were raised. By teaching them

well, and helping them develop a mindset that extends well beyond their immediate world, we can help them become actors on the global stage.

- *Forge ahead.* Not all of your colleagues will embrace the fact that you are working hard to retool your practice. Change is harder for some people than others. (Just look at some of the characters in *Downton Abbey* after World War I—longing for the way life used to be but would never be again.) Keep forging ahead anyway. Even better, try to win over the tech-averse people in your life and get them on your side.

- *Be a leader.* Working at the forefront of technology integration will set you apart. It can be a springboard for you to become an influential educational leader and help motivate you to keep learning, no matter what the "next new thing" is.

- *Have faith.* You are smarter and more resourceful than you think. And once you gain momentum as a TechnoTeacher, there will be no stopping you. Have faith in yourself. We do.

As authors, we will not disappear. We may be a little worse for wear, but we will continue to root for you. We will soon recover from simultaneous ear and eye strain (Nic furiously typing away on the laptop while listening to the variable hiss of the baby monitor) and the culinary fiascos that took place in Jules's kitchen while she was upstairs rewriting a paragraph or two. (Last-minute saves of overflowing pots of boiling pasta have become her specialty.) Come join us and teachers from all over the world on our website (www.Techno Teachers.com). Tell us how your school year is going. What do you need to launch that Stellar Unit you have been meaning to teach? What wisdom do you have to share with other TechnoTeachers? Let us hear from you. By working together, we will ensure that we become the best teachers we can be for the next generation. We are the TechnoTeachers.

TechnoTeaching Resources

RESOURCES BY CATEGORY

Alternative Forms of Recording
- http://www.youtube.com/watch?v=nmI_ne7sG5s
- http://www.youtube.com/watch?v=aetleFG7N4o

Cross-Cultural Online Exchanges
- James A. Bellanca and Terry Stirling, *Classrooms Without Borders: Using Internet Projects to Teach Communication and Collaboration* (New York: Teachers College Press, 2011).

Digital Project Management
- iGoogle (www.google.com/ig)
- My Yahoo! (http://my.yahoo.com)
- Netvibes (www.netvibes.com)

E-portfolios
- National Educational Technology Standards Electronic Portfolio Templates (http://electronicportfolios.org/nets.html). This ISTE site offers free templates to help you create your own e-portfolio using Word, Excel, PowerPoint, and HTML.

- Teacher Tap (http://www.eduscapes.com/tap/topic82.htm).

Podcasts

- To learn how to create a podcast, watch Australian educator David Fagg's tutorial (http://ihistory.wordpress.com/podcasts/how-do-i-make-a-podcast).
- For ideas on using podcasts in education, visit Wesley Fryer's Teach Digital website (http://teachdigital.pbwiki.com/podcasting).
- For ideas from Suzie Boss and Jane Krauss on how to incorporate technology more effectively into project-based learning activities, see http://player.fm/series/istes-podcast/iste-books-author-interview-episode-14-suzie-boss-and-jane-krauss. ISTE also has several helpful podcasts from other edtech enthusiasts; see http://player.fm/series/istes-podcast.
- To share your podcasts, try SoundCloud (https://soundcloud.com/).

Rubric Generators

- Intel Education's Assessing Projects Tool (https://educate.intel.com/en/AssessingProjects). See also teacher-generated rubrics at this site.
- RubiStar (http://rubistar.4teachers.org).

Skyping with Authors

- John Micklos Jr., "Authors Who Skype: A New Way to Stimulate Student Reading," *Reading Today* 29, no. 6 (June/July 2012): 22–23, http://www.reading.org.
- http://www.katemessner.com/authors-who-skype-with-classes-book-clubs-for-free
- http://skypeanauthor.wetpaint.com
- http://www.skypeauthors.com

Wikis

- PBwiki (http://pbworks.com/)
- Wikispaces (http://www.wikispaces.com/content/teacher/)

ADDITIONAL RESOURCES BY NAME

- *BoomWriter (www.boomwriter.com).* Given a first chapter, or "story start," students work in groups to write the subsequent chapters of storybooks and then vote online for the best one. The winning chapter is published. This is a great way to get students writing together in groups.
- *BrainPop (www.brainpop.com).* This is a subscription-based Web site with animated curricular content for individual, team, and whole-class learning. A Spanish version is also available.
- *Edmodo (www.edmodo.com).* This social learning platform—a bit like a super educational Facebook—includes features such as "Measure Student Progress" and "Connect to Resources" to help you build your online community.
- *Edublogs (http://edublogs.com).* This popular global educational blogging service is easy to use and set up class accounts. Initial setup is free.
- *EdWeb (www.edweb.net).* Search here for free webinars on a range of educational topics, as well as special interest group chats.
- *Glogster (www.glogster.com/).* This site introduces an exciting new way of creating a presentation—part mood board, part blog.
- *GoAnimate (http://goanimate4schools.com).* This DIY video site walks you though drag-and-drop video creation. It is not free, but it's very engaging for both staff and students!
- *International Society for Technology in Education special interest groups (http://www.iste.org/connect/special-interest-groups).* Check out the SIGs (twenty-one as of this writing), professional development opportunities, and discussion forums available through ISTE.
- *MeetUp (www.meetup.com).* Use this social media tool to find special interest groups in your area. Click "Education and Learning" to see if there's a group that interests you.
- *Prezi (www.prezi.com/prezi-for-education).* This site offers an alternative to Microsoft PowerPoint. Be wary of new users who can create

presentations that make the audience seasick with all the zooming in and out!

- *Skype in the Classroom (http://education.skype.com).* This free resource enables teachers to develop a global community of educators focused on particular projects.
- *SlideRocket (www.sliderocket.com).* This site (an alternative to SlideShare, listed next) offers presentation software that allows you to create and share presentations online.
- *SlideShare (www.slideshare.net/featured/category/ education).* Professionals, conference organizers, and schools can use this site to create and share presentations online—for free.
- *Vimeo (www.vimeo.com).* This video sharing site is free to upload and access. It's a favorite of teachers because it is not blocked by school firewalls as much as YouTube. Many also believe that its image and audio quality are far superior to YouTube's.
- *Voki (www.voki.com).* This free service lets you create avatars (little characters you can create dialogue for and add to blogs and Web sites— very stylish, but make sure you have substance too!). The site also includes lesson plans and tips.
- *YouTube (www.youtube.com).* This global giant site is used for uploading and downloading videos of just about anything.

Notes

INTRODUCTION

1. Common Core State Standards Initiative, "English Language Arts Standards, Introduction," http://www.corestandards.org/ELA-Literacy/introduction/students-who-are-college-and-career-ready-in-reading-writing-speaking-listening-language.
2. Barbara Means, William R. Peneul, and Zayidtina Padilla, *The Connected School* (San Francisco: Jossey-Bass, 2001).
3. Sherry Turkle, *Alone Together* (New York: Basic Books, 2011), xii.
4. For more on the downside of technology, see Alex Soojung-Kim Pang, *The Distraction Addiction* (New York: Little, Brown and Company, 2013); Catherine Steiner-Adair with Teresa H. Barker, *The Big Disconnect* (New York: HarperCollins, 2013); and Howard Gardner and Katie Davis, *The App Generation* (New Haven, CT: Yale University Press, 2013). All were mentioned in Dwight Gardner, "Resisting the Siren Call of the Screen," *New York Times,* August 19, 2013, C1 and C4.
5. Sir Tim Berners-Lee, "The Evolution of the Internet" (paper presented at the American Academy of Arts & Sciences, Cambridge, Massachusetts, Spring 2013).

CHAPTER 1

1. Judith Sandholtz, Cathy Ringstaff, and David C. Dwyer, *Changing the Conversation About Teaching Learning & Technology: A Report on 10 Years of ACOT Research* (Cupertino, CA: Apple, Inc., 1995), http://imet.csus.edu/imet1/baeza/PDF%20Files/Upload/10yr.pdf.
2. Judith Sandholtz, Cathy Ringstaff, and David C. Dwyer, *Teaching with Technology: Creating Student-Centered Classrooms* (New York: Teachers College, 1997), 42–43.
3. Check out the Video Blocks website for inspiration (a time-lapse video of London's Tower Bridge or a lightning storm over a country field), at http://www.videoblocks.com/videos/time-lapse.
4. See http://www.dartfish.com/en/education_software/physical-education.htm.
5. Sandholtz, Ringstaff, and Dwyer, *Teaching with Technology,* 44–47.
6. Julie M. Wood, "Early Literacy Instruction and Educational Technologies: Three Classroom-Based Models" (EdD dissertation, Harvard Graduate School of Education, 1999).
7. Howard Gardner, "Extraordinary Minds" (paper presented at the Harvard Graduate School of Education, Cambridge, Massachusetts, May 6, 1998).
8. Howard Gardner, *Leading Minds* (New York: HarperCollins, 1995), 10.

9. Andrew Hargreaves and Michael Fullan in "The Power of Professional Capital," *Journal of Staff Development* 34 (June 2013): 39, www.learningforward.org.

10. Sandholtz, Ringstaff, and Dwyer, *Teaching with Technology*.

11. See www.iste.org and www.reading.org, respectively.

12. For a free copy of the International Reading Association's position paper "New Literacies and 21st-Century Technologies," see http://www.reading.org/general/AboutIRA/Position Statements/21stCenturyLiteracies.aspx.

13. See www.weebly.com.

CHAPTER 2

1. In subsequent chapters, Nic will share the tricks of the trade she has developed over the years for finding the time, energy, and resources you need to realize your goals.

CHAPTER 3

1. Phil Johnson, "Sir Ken Robinson Urges Us to Find Our Passions, Question Our Limitations," *The Council Chronicle* 22, no. 2 (2012).

2. Common Core State Standards Initiative, "English Language Arts Standards, Introduction," http://www.corestandards.org/ELA-Literacy/introduction/students-who-are-college-and-career-ready-in-reading-writing-speaking-listening-language.

3. Ibid.

4. See www.pbslearningmedia.org/.

5. Ralph Fletcher and JoAnn Portalupi, *Writing Workshop: The Essential Guide* (Portsmouth, NH: Heinemann, 2001), 103.

6. Write: Outloud and Co:Writer are both published by Don Johnston (www.donjohnston.com). Dragon Dictate is published by NanoPac (www.nanopac.com).

7. James M. Cooper, ed., *Classroom Teaching Skills*, 7th edition (Boston: Houghton Mifflin, 2003), 295–296.

8. Monica Burns, "Four Free Assessment Apps for 1:1 Classrooms," Edutopia.org Assessment blog, January 4, 2013, www.edutopia.org/blog/free-assessment-ipad-apps-monica-burns.

9. Interview with Deborah McDevitt, Director of Social Studies, Belmont High School, Belmont, Massachusetts, on location, January 17, 2013.

10. Nonie K. Lesaux and Sky H. Marietta, *Making Assessment Matter* (New York: Guilford Press, 2012), 31.

11. Rebecca Alber, "Deeper Learning: Defining Twenty-First Century Literacy," Edutopia.org, January 21, 2013, http://www.edutopia.org/blog/twenty-first-century-literacy-deeper-learning-rebecca-alber.

12. Monica Burns, "Score Rubrics on Your iPad," Class Tech Tips blog, February 11, 2013, http://classtechtips.com/2013/02/11/grade-rubrics-on-your-ipad/.

13. "Louise Maine on Wikis," YouTube video, posted by Edutopia.org, May 22, 2012, http://www.youtube.com/watch?v = MtQHOdh2baU.

14. Danielle Nicole DeVoss, Elyse Eidman-Aadahl, and Troy Hicks, *Because Digital Writing Matters* (San Francisco: Jossey-Bass, 2010), 49–53.

CHAPTER 4

1. To make your own digital calendar, go to www.google.com/googlecalendar/overview.html.
2. Research, for example, by Nancy Farnan and Leif Fearn, "Writing in the Disciplines: More Than Writing Across the Curriculum," in *Content Area Reading and Learning: Instructional Strategies,* 3rd ed., ed. Diane Lapp, James Flood, and Nancy Farnan (New York: Erlbaum, 2008), 403–423.
3. Steve Graham, Charles A. MacArthur, and Jill Fitzgerald, *Best Practices in Writing Instruction,* 2nd ed. (New York: Guilford Press).
4. For a more elaborate unit on graphic organizers, see Thomas DeVere Wolsey and Dana L. Grisham, *Transforming Writing Instruction in the Digital Age* (New York: Guilford Press, 2012), 147–151.
5. You can find graphic organizers at ReadWriteThink (www.readwritethink.org/student_mat/index.asp) and ThinkingMaps (www.thinkingmaps.com). You can also use software such as Inspiration (www.inspiration.com) and SmartDraw (www.smartdraw.com).
6. www.planboardapp.com.

CHAPTER 5

1. "Good" and "Outstanding" are part of the Office for Standards in Education, Children's Services and Skills (Ofsted), the official body for inspecting schools in the U.K., http://www.ofsted.gov.uk/resources/framework-for-school-inspection.
2. See www.adobe.com/software/flash/about for a free download.
3. For example, for help with your animation timeline, see www.youtube.com/watch?v = RZBt CP-UEks.
4. See http://www.adobe.com/education/k12/adobe-education-leaders.edu.html.
5. See http://edex.adobe.com/.
6. See MicroPoll (www.micropoll.com) and PollDaddy (www.polldaddy.com).
7. See www.teachfind.com/teachers-tv/better-learning-ict-online-communities-classroom.
8. See the Electronic Groovemaker at www.ikmultimedia.com/products/cat-view.php?C = family-groovemaker; for PraiseHymns, see https://itunes.apple.com/gb/app/praise hymns/id387810480?mt = 8.
9. See Audacity at http://audacity.sourceforge.net/.
10. See, for example, http://www.history.co.uk/this-day-in-history.html.
11. www.google.com.
12. See ScribbleMaps.com.
13. See Rough Guides (www.roughguides.com) and Trip Advisor (www.tripadvisor.com).
14. See https://education.skype.com/.

15. See http://www.kidsastronomy.com/stars.htm and http://www.bbc.co.uk/learning-zone/clips/the-sun-and-the-stars/13291.html.

16. See www.googleartproject.com.

17. See https://itunes.apple.com/gb/app/word-maker/id410266135?mt=8.

18. See www.poets.org/page.php/prmID/6.

19. See, for example, KidsAstronomy.com.

CHAPTER 6

1. Asia Society, "President Obama Calls for American Education System to Align with Global Economy," http://asiasociety.org/education/policy-initiatives/national-initiatives/president-obama-calls-american-education-system-al.

2. Marcelo M. Suárez-Orozco and Carolyn Sattin, "Introduction," in *Learning in the Global Era,* ed. Marcelo M. Suárez-Orozco (Berkeley, California: University of California Press, 2007), 37.

3. Fearghal Kelly, "Online Communities Are Transforming Professional Development for Teachers," *The Guardian,* February 7, 2013, http://www.guardian.co .uk/teacher-network/teacher-blog/2013/feb/07/online-communities-transforming-professional-development-teaching.

4. Ibid.

5. Ibid.

6. Common Sense Media, "Our Mission," www.commonsensemedia.org/about-us/our-mission.

7. Suárez-Orozco and Sattin, *Learning in the Global Era,* 7.

8. Ibid., 11.

9. Organization for Economic Co-operation and Development (OECD), *Education at a Glance 2005* (Paris: OECD, 2005).

10. Veronica Boix-Mansilla and Howard Gardner, "Nurturing Global Consciousness," in *Learning in the Global Era,* ed. Marcelo M. Suárez-Orozco (Berkeley, California: University of California Press, 2007), 58–59.

11. Ibid., 58–63.

12. Miniwatts Marketing Group, "Internet World Stats," http://www.internetworldstats.com/eu/uk.htm.

13. Edward Wyatt, "Most of U.S. Is Wired, but Millions Aren't Plugged In," *New York Times,* August 19, 2013, B1, www.nytimes.com/2013/08/19/technology/a-push-to-connect-millions-who-live-offline-to-the-internet.html.

14. Edward Wyatt, "F.C.C. Backs Plan to Update a Fund That Helps Connect Schools to the Internet," *New York Times,* July 20, 2013, B3, http://www.nytimes.com/2013/07/20/business/media/fcc-backs-plan-to-update-a-fund-that-helps-connect-schools-to-the-internet.html.

15. Sir Tim Berners-Lee, "The Evolution of the Internet" (paper presented at the American Academy of Arts & Sciences, Cambridge, Massachusetts, Spring 2013), 19.

16. Edudemic, "Around the World in Social Networking," http://edudemic.com/wp-content/uploads/2013/01/social-networking.jpg.

17. Ki Mae Heussner, "With Nearly 10M Members, Edmodo Goes Back to School with a New Vision," Gigaom, September 4, 2012, http://gigaom.com/2012/09/04/with-nearly-10m-members-edmodo-goes-back-to-school-with-new-version/.

18. See www.classroom20.com.

19. See edupln.ning.com.

20. See www.edX.org and www.coursera.org.

21. See englishcompanion.ning.com.

22. Quoted in Lorna Collier, "Capitalizing on Social Media," *Council Chronicle*, National Council of Teachers of English 21, no. 3 (March 2012): 27.

23. See www.curriki.org.

24. See www.pedagoo.org.

25. See www.guardian.co.uk/teacher-network.

26. See www.thinkfinity.org.

27. See www.readwritethink.org.

28. For more cultural misunderstandings about India, see "Common Myths and Misconceptions About India," Indians Abroad blog, http://www.theindiansabroad.com/2009/08/common-myths-misconceptions-india/.

29. See https://education.skype.com.

30. See more on Charles Leadbeater's personal site at http://www.charlesleadbeater.net/home.aspx and a video at http://www.ted.com/talks/charles_leadbeater_on_education.html.

31. Boix-Mansilla and Gardner, "Nurturing Global Consciousness," 62.

32. Fee-based; see www.epals.com.

33. Ibid.

34. Adina Popa, "Globally Connected Classrooms" (webinar sponsored by EdWeb.net, November 8, 2012).

35. See the Global Virtual Classroom (http://www.virtualclassroom.org) and click "GVC Clubhouse" for ideas.

36. See www.globalreadaloud.com.

37. See www.virtualclassroom.org/clubhouse.html#.URVrsKFxfaQ.

38. Some of these ideas were inspired by resources from the John Stanford International School, Seattle, Washington, www.edutopia.org/stw-global-competence-resources.

39. Julie Wood interview with Chad Detloff, technology integration specialist, Chadwick School, Los Angeles, CA, September 21, 2012.

40. Julie Wood interview with Lillie Marshall, humanities teacher, Boston Latin Academy, October 2, 2012. For more, see Ms. Marshall's websites www.AroundTheWorldL.com and www.TeachingTraveling.com.

CHAPTER 7

1. See www.eschoolnews.org/funding/.
2. See www.edutopia.org/blog/grants-fundraising-tech-integration-mary-beth-hertz.
3. See www.mcf.org/mcf/grant/writing.htm.
4. See www.grants4teachers.com.
5. See http://www.britishcouncil.org/learning-school-partnerships-programme-grid-mar 2011.pdf.
6. See http://www.british-study.com/teacher-training/comenius-funding.php.
7. See http://schoolsonline.britishcouncil.org/programmes-and-funding/linking-programmes-worldwide/connecting-classrooms/partnerships.
8. See www.britishcouncil.org/etwinning.
9. See www.edweb.net and http://www.ted.com/topics/education.
10. See www.brainpop.com.

CHAPTER 8

1. Donald A. Schön, *The Reflective Practitioner* (San Francisco: Jossey-Bass, 1987), 22.
2. John Dewey, How We Think: A Restatement of the Relation of Reflective Thinking to the Educative Process (Chicago: Henry Regnery and Co., 1933), 63.
3. Carl A. Grant and Kenneth M. Zeichner, "On Becoming a Reflective Teacher," in Carl A. Grant, *Preparing for Reflective Teaching* (Boston: Allyn & Bacon, 1984), 104, http://www.wou.edu/~girodm/foundations/Grant_and_Zeichner.pdf.
4. Ibid., 105.
5. Ibid.
6. Dewey, *How We Think*, 17.
7. Schön, *The Reflective Practitioner*.
8. Peter Scales, "The Reflective Teacher," in Peter Scales, *Teaching in the Lifelong Learning Sector* (Maidenhead, England: Open University Press, 2008), 11, http://www.mcgraw-hill.co.uk/openup/chapters/9780335222407.pdf.
9. Grant and Zeichner, "On Becoming," 108.
10. Scales, "The Reflective Teacher."
11. Jack C. Richards, "Towards Reflective Teaching," *The Teacher Trainer* 5, no. 3 (1991), http://www.tttjournal.co.uk/uploads/File/back_articles/Towards_Reflective_Teaching.pdf.

Acknowledgments

From Us Both

We have so many people to whom we are deeply grateful. Friends, colleagues, family members, and yes, even the Doubting Thomases who have challenged our beliefs about how to help children become fully literate in the digital age. You have all given us the courage we needed to organize our thinking on paper and send it out into the world.

But let's start on a crisp winter morning when Nancy Walser, our wonderful editor, and (our U.S. representative) Julie met for coffee and scones in Harvard Square. Nic and Jules had already met online. We had talked back and forth for hours, virtually, about students, media, the sagging economy in both the United States and the U.K., and the plight of teachers who are trying to get with the times but don't have the tools or resources they need. We were modest in those days. Our thoughts turned to cowriting a few blog posts or perhaps a short newsletter article if we were lucky.

Nancy was polite, but seemed only mildly interested as she sipped her coffee. No wonder—our ideas hadn't properly gelled. Then Julie blurted out, "You know, there's a book that's waiting to be written. Nicole and I could coauthor it. It's about looking at your school year, basically thirty-six weeks . . ." Julie went on to describe the book you are holding in your hands.

That's how we began, with Nancy's fine-tuned sensibilities and careful eye leading us every step of the way. Nancy was unwavering in her support, even when the rough draft we sent her was, well, *rough*. She inspired us. She poked around in the places where there were holes in our thinking. She showed us how to write ten times better than we did when we began. Thank you, Nancy, for being a Dare Devil from the start and giving us the opportunity. You have kept us on track (changes!) and made us much better writers than we could ever hope to be, in such a small amount of time. You hold a special place in our hearts.

From Jules

Coauthoring this book with Nicole has been one of the most exciting, rewarding, and hilarious experiences of my career. When we weren't agonizing over the manuscript, trying to arrange all of our ideas into a logical sequence, we were gently teasing each other about the way we spoke English. "My coauthor is someone who uses the word *fortnight* in casual conversation!" I remarked to my husband. Meanwhile I've mistakenly led Nicole to believe that American teachers have a bigger salary than those in the U.K. ("Oysters?!") and are obsessed with baseball (well, the Red Sox did just win the World Series, after all!). Thank you, Nicole, my best-ever buddy across the pond, for being the warm, original, witty woman you are. You are truly one of a kind. I am so glad the Fates contrived a way for us to meet in cyberspace. The odds were so against it.

As with every project I have ever done over the last twenty-five years, I have my brilliant husband, John, to thank. He has never ceased to inspire, challenge, and offer fresh perspectives. In his scientific career, he has cultivated the idea that the most interesting work often occurs at the intersection of two disciplines. That is how he made his mark. His philosophy must have rubbed off on me; to my thinking, the intersection of literacy and new technologies is where some of the most promising ideas about children and learning are emerging today. I love you, John. And someday you will be given the honorary degree in education you so richly deserve for having nurtured my writing over all these years.

Next, my wholehearted thanks to my writing group. Deborah Iles, Susan Larkin, Buzz Anderson, and Alex Baker, you have made being a writer the most enlightening and entertaining activity that those of us who love books and words can pursue. Our monthly meetings over nachos and wine sustain me. I live for our fictional characters, who hover over our table and lurk in doorways as we debate plot structure and whether they would really have said *that*. You have enriched my life. Julia Thacker, you are my muse.

Also, here's to some of the innovative teachers who have been generous with their time. You have let me interview you via Skype, in person, and over the phone. You are the real deal. My heartfelt thanks to Dan Riles, Kingsley Montessori School, Boston; Golriz Golkar, San Francisco; Robert Simpson, Brookline, Massachusetts; Sandy Beck, Cumming, Georgia; Michael King, Byfield, Massachusetts; Sean Breen, San Francisco; Mary Anton Oldenburg, Lexington, Massachusetts; Deborah Levy, Los Angeles; Chad Detloff, Palos Verdes Peninsula, California; Howard Wolke and Karen Hall, Lexington, Massachusetts; Lillie Marshall, Boston; Risa Carp, Deborah McDevitt, and Jeffrey Shea, Belmont, Massachusetts; and edtech blogger Margaret A. Powers, Philadelphia.

I have been lucky in life. I had the opportunity to begin my career teaching literacy skills to young children in a semirural town in New Hampshire. After several stops along the way—in educational publishing, children's media, and academia—here I am again, teaching young children in Boston. To all the teachers at the Kingsley Montessori School, you fill my days with joy and light and remind me why being an educator is one of the most rewarding careers a person can have. "Real success is finding your lifework in the work that you love," says author/historian David McCullough. Right on!

As another author, Anne Lamott, says, "Astonishing material and revelation appear in our lives all the time. Let it be. Unto us, so much is given. We just have to be open for business."

Let's be open for business together.

Julie M. Wood
Cambridge, Massachusetts, USA

From Nic

Some books evolve over years. In true testament to the fast-moving nature of the digital advances we like to promote, this book evolved over a ridiculously short period of time. Therefore, my first personal thank you is to my coauthor, the incredible force of nature that is Julie M. Wood. She put herself out there, took a chance on a Brit, and became so much more than a colleague throughout this process. She even sent my husband and me Harvard T-shirts so I knew it was all real.

Jules: you have been so understanding, from being there with kind words as I have learnt how to be a working mummy—Skyping during naptimes and e-mailing whilst cooking dinner—to taking on the lion's share of the final edits when we moved house, and just being . . . lovely. You are the most creative writer and passionate educator that I have "met"—online or off. You are an inspiration. I now consider you a very, very close friend—as well as the main name in my inbox! I only hope to meet you one day and give you a real cuddle for being so very brilliant.

Secondly, I want to let Richard Gent, the mastermind behind Edusites, know how much I appreciate his trust. From when I initially asked if he wanted a few of my old A-level resources, he invited me into his world, and encouraged me to *really* look at writing for a living. He really did make my dreams come true. Neither of us knew that a PR attempt would lead to Julie and me becoming writing chums. He opened a door for me and I will never forget this—thanks, Richard!

Next, I want to thank all the teachers (past and present) that I know. I have worked with Zayids, Melissas, and Jasmines in a number of schools, and continue to admire those in education in my role as a freelance consultant. Working for the charity Achievement for All, I have met and learnt from excellent colleagues and peers alike. My admiration for leadership teams, classroom teachers, and support staff is increased with each visit. My experience in U.K. schools gives me hope for education in this country, and for the next generations of digital learning, despite consistent cuts, poor morale, and constant pressure. We have heroes in the classroom who do incredible work every lesson. Teaching really is the noblest profession. I want to thank everyone who has supported me on this professional journey and has been happy to sweep up/ignore the odd smashed, spinning plate that has slipped from my grasp.

Being a working mother has meant that I have had to *lean* on a few people, and in particular, one of the hardest working mums I know: my mother. She has worked for as long as I can remember and is showing no signs of slowing down! I want to thank my mum, Marianne Abley, for being there, for looking after our little one with such tenderness, and for helping us to raise him whilst I have been hunched over this laptop. I couldn't have done this without you. Cheers, mum (and Ed!).

I also want to thank the Ponsford Seniors—Jo and Ray—for all they have done for us. This includes being there in the wings when needed, speeding down the M3 when a "red cross" has been painted on our door, and always being there with cakes and toy cars aplenty.

Normally, one would thank individuals who have been supportive on a day-to-day basis. This would be fellow teachers, but being a part-time worker/ mummy working online, I now want to thank my inner circle of friends and family, who have been there when I am offline. I want to thank my "mummy mates" and my "old" (ha!) school friends, who have made me repeat what I am doing *every time* they see me, give me a sense of balance, and have always been quick to send a text or Facebook comment to celebrate each step of this incredible journey. So, to my partner in crime (the one and only Nicola Jane C, and the Twinkles), "Aunty Gemma," Gaye, Parker, and CJ, Zip, Bri, Lucy of the Lombi, the Wickettes, Nade, the Hoyles, and the Ellums: I owe you one. A large one. Most of you have no idea what I am writing about and aren't too bothered about teaching, yet you have given me strength to keep typing. You all rule.

Now to my two favourite boys, the Ponsford Juniors—I love you both. I want to thank my gorgeous son for being the smile on my face and the joy in my heart. R-Star, you really are my son-shine. I'm so very proud of you.

And then to my best friend, David: you have not just supported Monkey and me through the preschool years—and *our* next chapter (in the "new home"), but you've also given me the freedom to chase my dreams. Your patience, your love, and the kindest eyes I have ever known have kept me going when I have been overwhelmed by it all. You never think you do enough, and yet you always put us first. You are my everything and the perfect husband. *It's all down to you, dear.* Here's to our next chapter.

Nicole Ponsford
Southbourne, Dorset, England

About the Authors

JULIE M. WOOD
Educational Consultant, Teacher, School Reformer, and Writer

An international educational consultant, Julie M. Wood, EdD, served as a faculty member and former director of the Jeanne Chall Reading Lab at the Harvard Graduate School of Education (HGSE), where she also earned a second master's degree in technology, innovation, and education and a doctorate in language and literacy. She also directed a HGSE-led comprehensive school reform initiative called Three to Third, aimed at helping to close the achievement gap for young children. As of the spring of 2013, she serves as the academic learning specialist at the Kingsley Montessori School in Boston.

Julie's writing has been featured in *Instructor* magazine, in *Scholastic Administrator*, on the *Teacher Radio* program (on Scholastic.com), on the PBS Expert site, and in the journal *Language Arts*. She has written chapters for an edited volume published by Harvard Education Letter (*The Digital Classroom*) and Harvard Education Press (*Better Teaching and Learning in the Digital Classroom*). Her book *Literacy Online* (Heinemann) expands upon these themes.

In addition, Julie has spoken at events, such as a forum on No Child Left Behind legislation at the Harvard University Law School; for organizations including the International Reading Association, National Council of Teachers of English, American Educational Research Association, and Texas Dyslexia Institute; and at international conferences.

A long-time educator, Julie began her career as a public school teacher and reading specialist. She has also served as a university lecturer, an editor/media developer in educational publishing, and a consultant on transmedia products for teachers and students. Her clients include Apple, Inc., Disney Interactive, Nickelodeon, Heinemann Publishers, HarperCollins, Houghton Mifflin, the U.S. Department of Education's Ready to Learn Partnership, and PBS Interactive, where she serves as the senior literacy advisor for new projects.

NICOLE PONSFORD
Educational Writer and Coach

Nicole Ponsford is an award-winning advanced skills teacher and former senior leadership team member who is now working as a freelance school improvement consultant and coach. She has worked in a variety of schools in the U.K., from leafy Surrey schools to inner-city academies, from "failing" to "outstanding" secondary schools. After developing a range of fourteen to nineteen subjects in multimedia, film, and the digital arts for adolescents, she moved on to advising principals, schools, local education authorities (LEAs), and national audiences.

Nicole has been nominated twice by her students and staff for the Teaching Awards, winning her first as "Outstanding New Teacher." She has been rated "Outstanding/1" several times as a teacher, head of department, and senior leader. She has worked with LEAs in the U.K. to transform services and change the way that education is delivered. Given her holistic view of education as a classroom practitioner and senior leader, as well as her experience as an A-level examiner/moderator and with creating networks for LEAs and advanced skills teachers, she offers a wealth of expertise in running curriculums, procuring resources, and raising standards in teaching and learning.

Her main current role is achievement coach for the international charity Achievement for All. In this position, Nicole works across the south of England to support accelerated progress in schools for the most vulnerable students across the school years. She has also worked with Early Support (reviewing its online resources and how they can be accessed by the public) and is part of a national case study involving schools and families who have school-age children with severe additional needs.

Nicole has written and edited a range of print and online material, including for the BBC and the General Teaching Council. She has worked with both national and international organizations to put digital learning and research at the heart of education (e.g., BSF, Vodafone, Apple, and Sony). Bringing together industry, charities, and schools, she has a passion for making pedagogy practical, looking toward the future of learning, and embracing emerging technologies. Nicole has written collaborative professional development (CPD) material for magazines and websites and has published work for international usage. She has mentored, coached, and led both teams and individuals in education, and is passionate about the future of teaching, supporting and developing teachers as professionals, and engaging students.

Index